Better Homes and Gardens.

celebrate the
SEASON
2010

table *of* contents

give from the heart

page 120 Surprise recipients with crafted and baked gifts they'll love. A handsome cribbage board, dainty jewelry box, and scrumptious chocolates are among this chapter's treasures.

inspire the kids

page 142 These fun-to-make items keep young ones busy doing what they love most —learning new techniques while making something they can call their own.

in a twinkling

These big-impact projects are easy on time and budget.

Better Homes and Gardens.

celebrate the SEASON 2010

Meredith Corporation Consumer Marketing
Vice President, Consumer Marketing: David Ball
Consumer Product Marketing Director: Steve Swanson
Consumer Product Marketing Manager: Wendy Merical
Business Manager: Ron Clingman
Associate Director, Production: Douglas M. Johnston
Photographers: Marty Baldwin, Jason Donnelley, Scott Little, Jay Wilde

Waterbury Publications, Inc.
Contributing Editor: Susan Banker
Contributing Graphic Designer: Catherine Brett
Editorial Director: Lisa Kingsley
Associate Editor: Tricia Laning
Creative Director: Ken Carlson
Associate Design Director: Doug Samuelson
Production Assistants: Kim Hopkins, Mindy Samuelson
Contributing Food Editor: Lois White
Contributing Food Stylist: Charles Worthington
Contributing Copy Editor: Terri Fredrickson
Contributing Proofreaders: Gretchen Kauffman, Peg Smith

***Better Homes and Gardens*® Magazine**
Editor in Chief: Gayle Goodson Butler
Art Director: Michael D. Belknap
Deputy Editor, Food and Entertaining: Nancy Wall Hopkins
Senior Food Editor: Richard Swearinger
Associate Food Editor: Erin Simpson
Editorial Assistant: Renee Irey

Meredith Publishing Group
President: Jack Griffin
Executive Vice President: Andy Sareyan
Vice President, Manufacturing: Bruce Heston

Meredith Corporation
Chairman of the Board: William T. Kerr
President and Chief Executive Officer: Stephen M. Lacy

In Memoriam: E.T. Meredith III (1933–2003)

All of us at Meredith Consumer Marketing are dedicated to
providing you with information and ideas to enhance your home.
We welcome your comments and suggestions. Write to us at:
Meredith Consumer Marketing, 1716 Locust Street,
Des Moines, IA 50309-3023.

joyful greetings

One of my most treasured Christmas rituals is setting aside a night to linger over the dozens of holiday cards that fill the handcrafted wood sleigh that my grandfather made nearly 50 years ago.

I wait for an evening when everyone else in the house is fast asleep. Surrounded by the twinkling of holiday lights and with a cup of hot cider by my side, I begin the anticipated ceremony.

One by one, I pull each card from its envelope. I lose myself in photos and letters that share the yearly highlights as well as the holiday plans of each family. These fun-to-read notes reiterate that holiday gatherings, decorating, and gift-giving are at the heart of what makes the season bright.

It's in recognition of these heartfelt sentiments that we bring you *Celebrate the Season 2010*, complete with dozens of festive trims for the autumn and winter seasons, incredible recipes to share, and wondrous gifts to make and give with pride.

We hope that in some small way the ideas and inspiration in the following pages add to your holiday traditions and fill you with the warmth and spirit of the season.

Happiest of holidays,

Sue Banker

Sue Banker

CELEBRATE
AUTUMN

Whether picked up on a
hike or purchased at the
local farmer's market,
autumn finds naturally lead
the way to the season's
finest decorating ideas.

bring in the outdoors

When the days turn cool, invite Mother Nature's bounty to the dining room table for a fresh-air atmosphere.

a natural winner

Blanket the table with autumnal colors and textures. A plain pumpkin makes the perfect centerpiece while pinecones topple across the pretty scene. Add flowers to the setting by placing a potted mum near the table.

corner cones

🍂 Pinecones with extravagant bows add special touches to tablecloth corners. To allow pinecones to hang properly, twist a small screw eye into the top of each pinecone. Fold up the tablecloth corner and use a safety pin poked through the screw eye to secure in place. Tie a bow made of natural fiber ribbon around the screw eye to hide the hardware.

age revival

🍂 Breathe new life into a printed tablecloth from days gone by. Choose a cloth that complements the season's colors and edge it in a coordinating plaid. Accent the design with a sprinkling of embroidery floss stitches, such as those on page 155.

lovely leaves

Favorite leaf shapes inspire this subtle etched plate and clay favor holder.

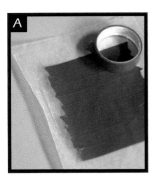

A

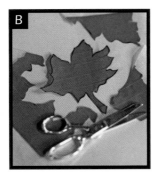

B

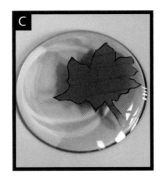

C

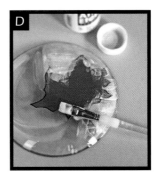

D

autumn etched plate

∿ Silhouette the most popular symbol of the season on a glass plate using an easy etching technique.

1   Tear off a piece of waxed paper approximately 8 inches wide. Cover a 5×7-inch area with rows of masking tape, overlapping the edge of the previously laid strip as shown in Photo A, above.

2   Enlarge and trace the leaf pattern, page 154, onto tracing paper; cut out. Trace around pattern on taped rectangle; cut out as shown in Photo B.

3   Carefully peel off waxed paper from masking tape. Press tape shape onto the back of a clean plate as shown in Photo C. Press edges firmly to the plate.

4   Follow the etching cream manufacturer's instructions to etch the plate as shown in Photo D. Rinse the plate thoroughly with water and remove the masking tape.

leaf favor holder

∿ Use the same pattern as for the etched leaf plate or use a large leaf to trace the shape.

1   Cover the work surface with waxed paper. Use a rolling pin to flatten clay to a ¼-inch thickness.

2   Tear off a piece of waxed paper and crumple it. Open up the paper and lay it over clay. Use the rolling pin to press the wrinkles of the paper into the clay surface as shown in Photo A, below. Remove the waxed paper.

3   Place the leaf or leaf pattern on the clay as shown in Photo B.

4   On a work surface covered with waxed paper, use a crafts knife to cut around leaf shape, leaving a thick stem so it does not break, as shown in Photo C.

5   Place a spoon upside down on a baking pan. Place the leaf, textured side down, on the spoon as shown in Photo D. Bake the clay in the oven following the manufacturer's instructions.

11

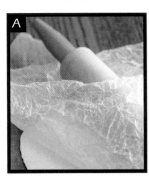

A

B

C

D

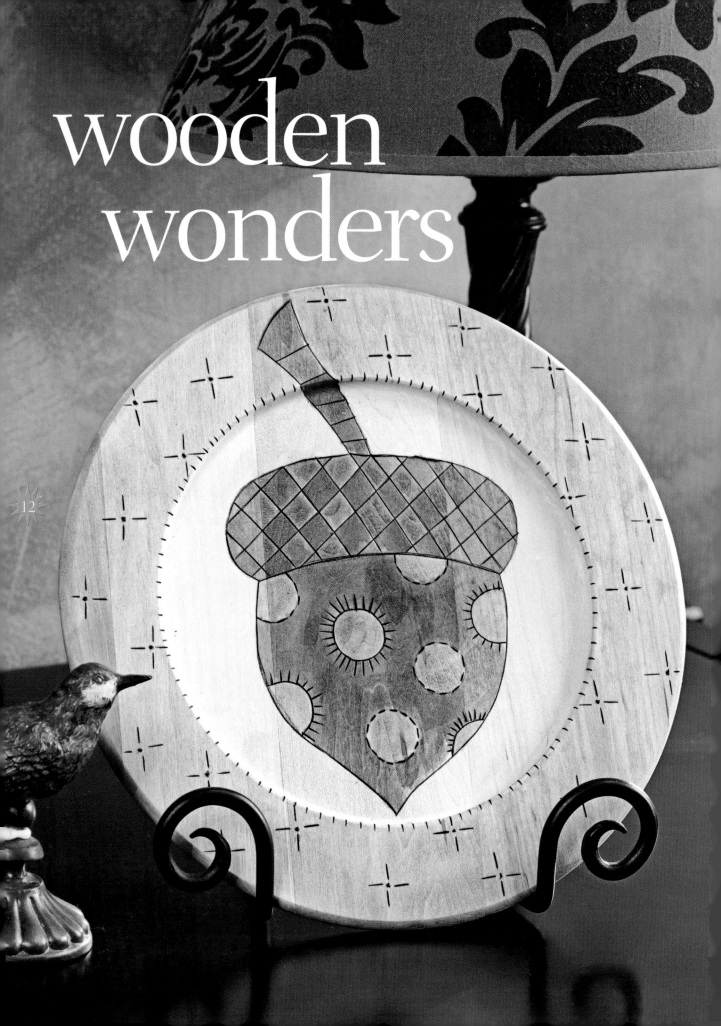

wooden wonders

12

Let the natural beauty of wood accompany fall decorating. Laced, woodburned, or creatively glued, these striking home accents are yet another way to bring the outdoors in.

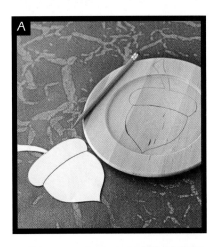

stylish acorn plate

∽ Even beginning woodburners can master this decorative plate with ease. Stain in natural hues details the design.

What You'll Need...
- tracing paper
- pencil
- scissors
- 12-inch wood plate
- penny
- woodburner
- wood stains in desired colors
- small artist's paintbrushes
- clear satin topcoat spray
- fine sandpaper, optional

1 Enlarge and trace the acorn pattern on page 154; cut out. Trace pattern on the center of the plate as shown in Photo A, right.

2 Using the photo as a guide, trace around a penny to make dots in the bottom portion of the acorn as shown in Photo B. Be sure to burn in deeply enough so the stain does not bleed.

3 Following the manufacturer's directions, woodburn the outline of the acorn as shown in Photo C.

4 Make dotted lines or starburst designs around each circle as shown in Photo D.

5 Woodburn uneven stripes into the stem, crosshatches into the cap, marks along the inner edge of the plate rim, and a simple cross with center dot designs around the rim.

6 Using the woodburned lines as guides and the photo for inspiration, brush in the areas of the design using the desired colors of stain. Be careful to stay within the burned lines so the stain does not bleed. Let dry.

7 Spray the plate with one or more coats of clear satin spray, allowing to dry and lightly sanding between coats if needed for smoothness. Let dry.

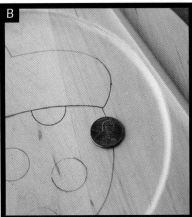

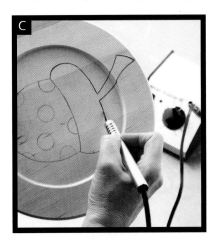

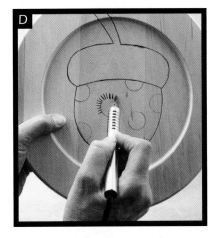

14

rim trim

Soft leather lacing dresses up a wood bowl in short time. Simply mark and drill evenly spaced holes ¹/₂ inch from the lip of the bowl to make way for the leather trim.

classy coasters

Small wood embellishments march in rows to create modern coasters. Turn to hardware and crafts stores to find an assortment of small wooden pieces. Arrange them on a 4-inch square of wood to create a coaster. Be sure the surface is level enough to hold glasses upright before hot-gluing the pieces in place.

woodsy photo frame

A trek through the woods is all it takes to gather a few fallen finds to deck out a frame. Acorn caps and small pinecones arranged in artistic symmetry transform a plain frame into a clever creation perfect for any lodge lover.

picture it

With a purchased wood slice as the background, this autumn scene can be created in minutes. Hot-glue six sticks in place as shown, finishing the floral-inspired design with acorn parts and mini pinecones.

tray chic

∿ A wooden tray edged with jute makes the perfect resting spot for a selection of speckled cobs. Tie the husks with rust color ribbon to complete the lovely arrangement.

center of attention

∿ Corn nestles on a bed of wheat for a feast of earthy color and texture that's distinctly fall. Some of the husks are removed to expose the kernels.

sun-kissed sensation

∿ This ear of corn has a shimmery secret: It was brushed with metallic dusting powder from a cake decorator's tool kit. A name tag threaded with narrow ribbon turns it into a personalized place card.

fall field day

Colorful Indian corn is interesting all by itself. Embellished with ribbon, rope, and wheat, it becomes the show stealer on any tabletop

18

seasonal sunburst

For an easy decoration that lasts year to year, cover an 8-inch straw wreath form in corn husks. Add husks one by one, spreading hot glue on the bottom half of the husk and wrapping it around the wreath from back to front. Repeat until the form is covered.

autumn glow

Fashion a footlight by standing a solar-powered light stake in a generous size pot then snuggling ears of full-size corn around it. Leaving husks attached to the ends keeps the ears upright.

great garland

To decorate a fence, cut rope 2 feet longer than the fence. Twist one screw eye hook (with an opening about the size of the rope) into the top of each mini ear of corn. Bend husks into loops and hot-glue the pointed ends together. Thread the husks and ears onto the rope and hang.

pleasant surprise

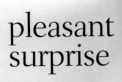 Dress up an autumn tabletop easily with an ear of corn snuggled into a cloth napkin. A short length of braid holds the duo in place.

22

light play

To make these husk-wrapped votive holders begin with a package of uniform, clean, pressed grocery-store tamale husks. Soak a husk in warm water for 1 minute to make it pliable, then wrap it tightly around a votive holder and secure with a rubber band. Trim excess at top and bottom. Tie a narrow strip of twisted husk around the center of the votive and remove the rubber band.

24

and smiles

Celebrate Thanksgiving with surprising trims and a touch of humor. It is a fun way to brighten your home during the season of thanks.

color bursts

 Unexpected tones of pink, turquoise, and olive green pop against a luscious palette of pumpkin orange. Look closely to witness out-of-season daisies blooming alongside traditional Thanksgiving trims.

dotted with daisies

Bands of print ribbons pin easily to a pumpkin to add a quick surprising touch. Whimsical paper daisies made from a punch playfully dot the surface.

26

tina turkey

Turkeys aren't just named Tom anymore! This fancy fowl donning high heels and floral feathers will make Thanksgiving guests giggle.

What You'll Need...

- [ ] tracing paper
- [ ] pencil
- [ ] scissors
- [ ] card stock in shades of orange, red, brown, and gold
- [ ] glue stick
- [ ] card stock scraps in white, blue, purple, and black
- [ ] flower paper punch
- [ ] 12-inch square of card stock
- [ ] desired mat and frame

1. Enlarge and trace the patterns on page 154; cut out. Use patterns to cut pieces from desired colors of card stock.

2. Arrange feathers in desired order. Punch several flowers from every other feather. Back each cutout with a contrasting feather cutout; glue together.

3. Use the paper punch to punch flower centers. Glue to flower centers.

4. Fan out and glue the feathers to the square background, 1 inch from the top edge.

5. If desired, glue the body, wing, wattle, and head to contrasting pieces of card stock. Trim around pieces, leaving a narrow border. Repeat if desired. Using the photo for inspiration, glue the pieces together

6. Arrange and glue the body pieces to the feathers. Punch small dots and glue in place to accent eyes and shoes.

7. Frame as desired.

flowerpot favor

Treat Thanksgiving guests to a cupful of candy nested in a natural pod. Match petal ribbons to those used on the pumpkin centerpiece.

What You'll Need...

- [ ] 6-inch-long pieces of 1-inch-wide ribbon
- [ ] stapler
- [ ] hot-glue gun and glue sticks
- [ ] pod on wire stem
- [ ] mini flowerpot
- [ ] candy cup
- [ ] corn kernels
- [ ] small candies

1. Bring the ends of each ribbon piece together; staple. Arranging the ribbon pieces as petals on a flower, hot-glue the stapled ends to the underside of the pod.

2. Cut the wire stem 4 inches longer than desired height. Shape the wire end in a flat coil to fit into flowerpot bottom; hot-glue in place.

3. Hot-glue a candy cup in the pod opening. Fill the flowerpot with corn kernels; place candies in candy cup.

27

up and running

For just a few dollars, you can treat your fall table to a new runner. Cut prewashed burlap to size and use a T-pin to separate and remove threads, making an inch of fringe on all sides. Hot-glue on a border of wide flat trim.

textural appeal

Good old burlap—handsome, versatile, and outrageously affordable —is the perfect fabric for no-sew projects all around the house.

welcome mats

Blond frames with burlap mats unify an artwork collection. To cover mat, cut burlap 2 inches larger than mat. Center mat on burlap and cut an X in the opening to each corner. Wrap flaps around the mat edges and hot-glue in place; trim excess fabric.

nesting place ▶

A full twig wreath is sturdy enough to hold even the largest gourds. If the gourds tend to topple, use an ice pick to poke holes in them, then use wire to attach the gourds to the branches.

In a Twinkling
gorgeous gourds

◀ **stacked simplicity**

Stack a gourd on a stemless one for a pretty pair. Wrap the mini mound package-style using jute twine, tying the ends in a bow around the top gourd's stem.

▼ **picturesque place setting**

Top dinnerware with a gourd that boasts a name tag. A simple leaf shape cut from green art paper and threaded on jute welcomes each guest to the table.

vintage introductions
Aged tins create an interesting
landscape for showcasing a
gathering of gourds. If
needed, use poster putty to
hold the gourds in place.

31

beauty and the box
A wooden box is a natural
landing spot for a collection
of small gourds. Enhance the
look with a few sprigs of
wheat towering over the
colorful arrangement.

▲ **colorful throne**
Dried and silk autumn flowers make a striking
platform to hold a single gourd. Start with a
wood circle base and hot-glue the trims in
place to create a symmetrical pattern.

DECK *the* HALLS

Spread holiday cheer
throughout your home
with festive trimmings
that suit the season.

dressing up the

cool collection

Holiday cookie jars are a wonderful way to decorate above kitchen cupboards. If you don't have display room there, let your collection march down the center of the table or place them strategically around the counters.

hub

When guests migrate to the kitchen at Christmastime, welcome all with jolly displays and special take-home treats.

island getaway

Make the kitchen island guest-friendly by covering it with a cheery tablecloth. Keep trims to the center of the station, allowing resting places for food and drinks.

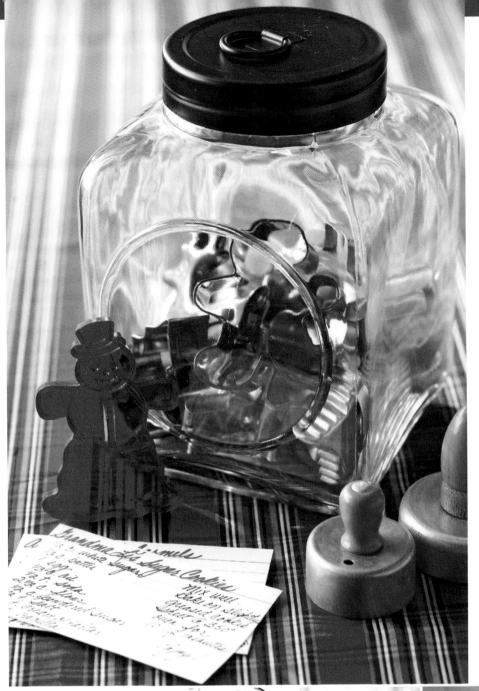

cookie cutter display

❧ No need to hide holiday cookie cutters in the pantry. Keep them in a large glass jar, pulling out a few favorites to highlight. Make copies of favorite holiday cookie recipes to share with guests.

time for fun

❧ A wall clock gets oodles of attention propped proudly on a tabletop easel. Use crafts wire to attach a holiday pick of greenery, pinecones, and small ornaments, then tie on a ribbon bow for the finishing touch.

goblet markers

❧ Circle makers cut out these handy stemware I.D.s in a hurry. Use the cutters to make two slightly different sizes of donut shapes to fit stemware. Use a snowflake punch to create a design at the edge of the top layer. Glue the donut shapes together and cut a slit opposite the snowflake to slip around the glass stem.

the giving tree

Trim a tabletop tree with home-baked goodies, such as cookies and candies, to share with holiday visitors. Decorated with bright punches of color and striking black and white, these take-aways are sure to be a hit.

jolly jars

✑ To make festive candy holders, etch small jars and accent them with small bunches of wired pinecones and berries tied with ribbon. For a perfect caramel recipe, see page 136.

What You'll Need...

- [ ] small glass jars
- [ ] paper reinforcements
- [ ] paintbrush
- [ ] etching cream
- [ ] narrow ribbon
- [ ] wired pinecones
- [ ] wired artificial berries
- [ ] chenille stems
- [ ] hot-glue gun and glue sticks

1. Place the circular reinforcements randomly on the outside of the jar.

2. Following the manufacturer's directions, brush etching cream onto the entire outside of the jar, including the bottom. Allow the cream to etch the glass then rinse off with water; let dry.

3. Tie a bow around a small arrangement of pinecones and berries.

4. Twist two chenille stems together to connect them approximately 1 inch from the ends. Split apart the stems and wrap them around the jar top just below the ridges. Twist the long ends together tightly to hold the jar. Continue twisting the stems together to make the handle. Secure the handle by twisting the ends with the 1-inch stem tails.

5. Hot-glue the pinecone sprig on top of the chenille stem ends.

sweet sensations

✑ Cookies slipped into clear plastic bags and tied with a bow hang on the branches with ease. If desired, have copies of your recipes ready to share.

musical renditon

Accordion-folded holiday sheet music creates a graphic focal point on this wreath. For the bow center, wind and hot-glue decorative cord to a round napkin holder. Thread an additional piece of cord through the center and hot-glue a large jingle bell to each end. Tuck the folded sheet music through the ring and bend it into bow shape.

bows for boughs

Wreaths of greenery sing with style simply by adding stunning bows.

pretty pick

❧ Choose holiday picks of artificial berries and trims in various colors and styles along with coordinating ribbon to suit your decorating style. Tie a bow on the wreath and tuck in three picks to surround it.

beribboned beauty

❧ Check out this pretty bow before you toss away ribbon remnants. Using 12- to 18-inch lengths of ribbon, bring the cut ends together and wrap with wire to secure. Join the wound ends of several ribbon loops together to make the bow.

purely ornamental

❧ A trio of Christmas tree balls grabs attention when wired in a cluster. Accent the arrangement with loops of trim tucked behind.

All is calm when you deck
the halls with simplified
trims in neutral tones.

ah, natural

worldly gifts

For natural beauty,
wrap packages in smooth
white handmade paper
then trim with bands of
raffia-woven papers and
ties. Top the treasures
with naturals tucked into
the ties.

star of wonder

A bejeweled star
bordered in metallic thread
crowns a tree majesticly.
Cut a simple star shape
from stiff natural paper,
laminating it if needed for
stability. Add sparkle with
acrylic gem brads.

write on

Write holiday
sentiments or draw
super-simple motifs on a
solid-color ornament ball
using a puff-paint pen. To
display the pretty ornament,
nestle it in a weathered
moss-lined urn.

fresh start

A green and winter-white color scheme whispers "Christmas." Potted or cut, flowers and plants bring a sense of freshness to the table. Enhace the elegant scene with touches of silver.

44

button, button

❧ Assemble the buttons from your own collection or those you find at flea markets to make a charming wreath to hang over a doorknob. Cover a small straw wreath by wrapping it with white fabric or wide white ribbon. Sew different sizes and shapes of buttons to the fabric, varying the thread colors and using narrow ribbon to attach some.

45

seasonal smooching

❧ A strategically placed kissing ball seals the holidays with a kiss. Dress an ample-size topiary sphere with living needlepoint ivy. Wrap generous lengths of gold-edge sheer ribbon around the ball and tie it into soft bows with cascading trails. Tie a gold bell and ribbon bow to the base of the kissing ball. Then hang it where loved ones pass.

festive felt

A treasured fabric for crafters and sewing fanatics alike, felt makes its way into holiday decorating with vim and vigor.

branching out

❧ Felt scraps transform into a package topper with a few squirts of hot glue and a series of snips. To make a greenery sprig, cut an 8×4-inch piece of green felt. Fold it in half lengthwise. Hot-glue a 12-inch-long florist's wire to the center fold, aligning wire and felt at one end. Fold the felt in half to secure around the wire. Trim the felt on the aligned end to a point. Curl the remaining wire end into a loop. Create as many branches as desired and tie with a 12×2-inch length of felt; trim the ends to resemble a bow.

under cover

Personalize a holiday book or album with a felt cover. For simplicity, use a single silhouette, such as a cookie-cutter reindeer—perfect for a book about Rudolph. Cut felt wider than the open book. Wrap the ends around both covers; bond the edges with glue. Glue on the cutout deer, wrapping the body portion to the back.

47

jolly pair

ᑐᗑ Two familiar faces bring personality to evergreen branches. Make the easy-to-stitch ornaments by the dozens to give as gifts.

What You'll Need...
- [ ] tracing paper
- [ ] pencil
- [ ] paper
- [ ] felt in white, black, bright and pastel pink, red, purple, black, and orange
- [ ] embroidery floss in white and desired colors
- [ ] sewing needle
- [ ] fiberfill
- [ ] coordinating velvet ribbon

1 Trace ornament patterns on page 155; cut out. Using the photo as a guide, use patterns to cut felt pieces.

2 For snowman, use straight and cross stitches to attach the face pieces. Layer and sew hat brim to hat backing and snowman face; fringe the top edge of the brim.

3 Cut a 1×6-inch piece for scarf and two 1×1-inch pieces for contrasting fringe. Fold strip in half to make scarf. Tuck it between ornament front and back. Stitch along outer edge. Before closing, gently stuff with fiberfill. Stitch opening closed.

4 Stitch end pieces to scarf; fringe.

5 For the Santa, use straight and cross stitches to attach the face pieces, mustache, and beard. Layer and sew the hat brim to the hat backing and Santa face.

6 Stitch the ornament around the edge, leaving an opening for stuffing. Gently stuff with fiberfill. Stitch opening closed. Sew a ribbon hanger to the ornament top; tie with a ribbon bow.

circles and stripes

ᑐᗑ Freeform stitches make this stocking a nonsewer's dream.

What You'll Need...
- [ ] tracing paper
- [ ] pencil
- [ ] scissors
- [ ] ½ yard green felt
- [ ] 6×10-inch piece of blue felt
- [ ] felt scraps in red, pink, and purple
- [ ] white thread
- [ ] straight pins

1 Trace the stocking, cuff, and circle patterns on page 157. Use the patterns to cut 2 stocking pieces, 1 cuff, and 6 circles.

2 Using a zigzag stitch around the edges, sew the circles to the stocking cuff. Place the cuff on the stocking front, pin in place, and using machine straight stitches, crazy stitch the entire cuff area.

3 Machine stitch unparallel stripes across the stocking front.

4 Place the stocking pieces together and machine zigzag around the stocking, leaving the top open.

tradition
with a twist

The classic velvety-red poinsettia, still the favorite of traditionalists, has been joined by varieties of colors—coral, pink, plum, and cream. Welcome any of these beauties into your home this holiday season.

jingle bell rock

🎵 Give poinsettias an update—jingle bell centers that sparkle with holiday spirit. Add firm crafts wire "stems" to each bell, twisting them together in trios. Poke a grouping into the center of each bloom.

wreathed in blooms

🎵 Jazz up a myrtle wreath with three poinsettias in florist's picks. The variety 'Jingle Bells' is red, splashed with pink. Display the wreath indoors or choose artificial blooms for an outdoor decoration.

o christmas tree

Two-tone 'Strawberries 'n Cream' poinsettias become the ornaments on a potted treeform topiary of English ivy. Cut the flowers with about 6 inches of stem and remove the foliage. Place the cut poinsettias in a vase of cool water for 30 minutes to allow the cut ends to seal. Then poke each stem into a water-filled florist's pick and nestle it into the ivy.

dinner companion

∿ Mini 'Star' poinsettias are grown one flower per plant in a tiny plastic pot. Tucked into an espresso-size cup, they're a fine embellishment for a place setting.

by the chimney with care

∿ Pink-and-cream variegated petal poinsettias, cut and arranged one or two stems per vessel, bring cheer to a collection of white pottery on a fireplace mantel.

cranberry bouquet

∿ Cut a bouquet of ivory-color poinsettias for a table centerpiece. Cranberries in the clear glass vase hold the stems in place. Mingle the blossoms with Christmas greenery if you wish.

right to the point

Trims are coming up olive green and burnished copper in this holiday scheme.

ring around the tree

 Prairie points in alternating hues of copper, light green, and champagne add dramatic detail to the round velveteen tree skirt. The points are created by folding squares of ribbon into triangles and stitching them to the edge of rust-color ribbon binding.

What You'll Need ...

- [ ] 1⅔ yards of 54-inch-wide celery green velveteen
- [ ] 1⅔ yards of 54-inch-wide tan linen
- [ ] pencil or disappearing-ink fabric-marking pen
- [ ] 5 yards of 5-inch-wide dark rust-color ribbon
- [ ] 4 yards each of 5-inch-wide ribbon in light green, copper, and champagne
- [ ] 3 yards of 1⅜-inch-wide lime green organza ribbon
- [ ] scissors
- [ ] straightedge

1 Cut a 54-inch square from velveteen. Fold the fabric in quarters with wrong sides facing out.

2 Tie a piece of string around a pencil or disappearing-ink fabric-marking pen

and pin the string to the folded square corner. Adjust the length of the string to 27 inches. Beginning at one edge and keeping the string taut, draw a quarter circle on the fabric as if drawing with a compass. Without unfolding the fabric, adjust the string to 3 inches long. Draw a second quarter circle on the fabric.

3 Cut along the lines through all four layers of the fabric.

4 Repeat this procedure with the tan linen to make a lining piece.

5 Unfold the green velveteen circle and the lining. Layer the pieces with right sides facing and use a straightedge and pencil or disappearing-ink fabric-marking pen to draw a straight line from the outer raw edges to the inner circle. Cut along the line through both layers.

6 Fold the dark rust-color ribbon in half lengthwise to make the binding; press matching raw edges; pin the rust-color ribbon binding to the outer edge of the green velveteen circle; baste in place.

7 Cut the green-, champagne-, and copper-color ribbons into approximately forty-two 10-inch-long pieces. Fold the pieces in half to measure 5 inches square. With right sides facing and raw edges aligned, pin the folded ribbons under the folded edge of the dark rust-color ribbon binding, overlapping the pieces slightly; sew in place.

8 Fold in the folded corners of each ribbon segment toward the center back to form a prairie point; hand-tack the folds to each other on the back of each prairie point.

9 Place the lining and velvet tree skirt together with right sides facing. Sew the pieces together along all raw edges, leaving an opening along one side; turn.

10 Cut six 16-inch lengths from lime green organza ribbon for the ties. Evenly space and pin the ribbons to the top of the skirt along the straight open edges, aligning one short end of each ribbon with the straight edge. Edge-stitch along the straight edges and around the inner circle, catching all the ribbons in stitching.

jingle all the way

Based on a traditional elongated shape, these stocking get an update with a mix of satin, sheer, and striped ribbons fashioned in accents, cuffs, and heel and toe patches. The velveteen stockings gain contemporary flair dressed with layered rows of ribbons and prairie points embellished with festive bells.

What You'll Need...

- ¾ yard of celery green velveteen
- ¾ yard of tan linen
- 6-inch-long strip of 1½-inch-wide lime green grosgrain ribbon
- needle and matching sewing thread

For the Striped Stocking

- ½ yard of 1½-inch-wide green stripe double-sided ribbon
- 1½ yards of 3-inch-wide celadon green satin ribbon
- 1⅓ yards of 1⅜-inch-wide lime green organza ribbon
- 5 gold jingle bells

For the Striped Heel and Toe Stocking

- 1½ yards of 7-inch-wide rust-and-copper stripe ribbon
- 3 gold jingle bells

NOTE: The stockings use any basic stocking pattern. If desired, a pattern can be modified by elongating the top and by narrowing the outer curve above the heel.

1 Draw a stocking pattern or use the one on page 158, modifying the pattern as desired; cut out.

2 Use the pattern to cut a stocking front and back, reversing one of the shapes, from celery green velveteen. Cut a matching lining front and back from tan linen. Cut a 6-inch strip from lime green ribbon for the hanging loop.

3 Follow instructions for each stocking to embellish.

4 With right sides facing, stitch the velveteen stocking front to the back, leaving the top edge open. Clip the curves; turn the stocking right side out.

5 Stitch the lining pieces together with the right sides facing, leaving the top edge open and an opening along the curved stocking edge for turning the pieces right side out.

6 For hanging loop, press under ½ inch on each long edge of the 6-inch-long lime green ribbon. Fold strip in half lengthwise, aligning pressed edges; press again. Sew pressed edges together opposite fold. Sew the loop to the top outside corner on the heel side of the velveteen stocking.

7 Trim the stockings, then place the stocking inside the lining with the right sides facing. Stitch the stocking and the lining together around the top edge. Turn the stocking to the right side through the opening and lip-stitch the lining opening closed. Topstitch the upper edge.

STRIPED STOCKING EMBELLISHMENT

1 Cut five 3-inch lengths from the green stripe ribbon. Fold each length into a prairie point by folding each end in toward the center.

2 Cut a 9-inch length from celadon green satin ribbon. Pin the prairie points under one long edge of the celadon green satin ribbon with the folded edges facing out; topstitch in place.

3 Topstitch the ribbon along the top edge of the stocking front.

4 Topstitch a 9-inch-long lime green ribbon on top of the point-trimmed band.

5 Topstitch ribbons in evenly spaced horizontal rows along the length of the stocking front, layering sheer ribbons on satin ribbons.

6 Sew a jingle bell to each point.

STRIPED HEEL AND TOE STOCKING EMBELLISHMENT

1 Cut two 4-inch lengths from the rust-and-copper stripe ribbon. Position ribbons on heel and toe of velveteen stocking front, extending the extra ribbon beyond the stocking edges; pin in place. Topstitch the ribbons in place along the inner edges and trim the excess ribbon even with the stocking front raw edges.

2 Cut three 14-inch-long pieces from rust-and-copper stripe ribbon. Fold each piece in half to make a 7-inch square. Fold the short ends in to form a triangle; baste along the long edge.

3 Pin the 3 triangle shapes to the top raw edges of the velveteen stocking front, overlapping as desired; sew along the top edge. Sew a jingle bell to each point.

57

beaded beauties

Little beads shimmer across greenery containers and ornaments.

bead-dazzling ornaments

~ With glittered tops and beaded bases, these fancy ornaments can be crafted to complement any color holiday decor.

1 Use a paintbrush to coat the top third of the ornament with decoupage medium, avoiding the hanger. While wet, sprinkle the glue with glitter.

2 Coat the remainder of the ornament with decoupage medium and sprinkle with bead mixture. Hang the ornament until glue dries.

holly holder

~ A plastic fence post cap goes undercover as a wall mount vase blanketed with seed beads. To make the holder, drill a hole on one side of the cap for hanging. Using a paintbrush, coat the cap in thick crafts glue and sprinkle with beads while wet. Let the glue dry. Tie on a contrasting ribbon for extra pizzazz.

simple sparkle

Easy adornments give purchased ornaments a special touch.

twinkle from within

ꞷ Clear glass ornaments sparkle with metallic dots cascading from the top. To make the design, dip the handle end of a small paintbrush into glass paint and dot several times starting just below the hanger. The dots from top to bottom will naturally get smaller. Once the paint is dry, remove the hanger and fill the clear orb with lightweight white beads that shimmer.

serene scene

ꞷ It takes just minutes to paint one-of-a-kind ornaments with snowy landscapes.

What You'll Need...

- ☐ matte ornaments in desired color
- ☐ glass paint, such as Liquitex Glossies, in white and red
- ☐ fine paintbrush
- ☐ white glitter

1 Using Photo A, below, as a guide, paint simple white tree shapes around the center of the ornament

2 Paint the bottom third of the ornament white as shown in Photo B. While paint is wet, sprinkle with glitter as shown in Photo C.

3 Add small dots of red randomly to branches to resemble cardinals from a distance as shown in Photo D. Let the paint dry.

seasonal silhouettes

Make a classic statement using crisp black and white to highlight familiar holiday motifs.

man of the hour

This season capture the profile of St. Nick with a simple motif to cut out and frame. Use the pattern on page 156 to cut the design from black card stock. Mount the cutout on white before framing.

62

no two alike

Have fun snipping snowflakes from medium-weight white paper. Mount the pretties on black card stock circles adhered to slightly larger ones cut from white glitter paper to create one-of-a-kind coasters.

berry nice

A wreath motif makes an interesting holiday card. Cut a donut shape for wreath and the patterns on page 156 for bow. Complete wreath by punching out berries and trim edges with irregular cuts. To make a bow, glue ends of bow strip to center. Wrap center piece around bow; glue ends together and ribbon tails on back.

freehand fresh

You don't have to be an artist to master simple holiday motifs and letters. Use a small paintbrush and black glass paint to embellish plain white ornaments. Keep the designs simple for eyecatching silhouettes.

great plate

❧ Deck out each place setting with a striking black and white tree. To make the black tree, use the pattern on page 157 to cut the piece from folded card stock. While piece is folded, a paper punch creates instant ornaments. Open the design and glue it to white card stock. Use scissors to trim a narrow border.

forest fancy

❧ These handsome place cards lend dimension to the table. Use the pattern on page 156 to cut two trees for each card. Glue the bottom tree flat to the place card front using a glue stick. Adhere only the fold of the top tree to the center of the flat tree. Use a black pen or rub-on lettering to personalize.

jolly holly

❧ Perfect for any size package, these holly leaves are defined with glitter along the edges and veins. Use the patterns on page 156 to cut the seasonal leaves. Outline the details using crafts glue and sprinkle with glitter.

seashell cherubs

Lion's paw shells are a natural start to making these precious ornaments. Hot-glue a small wood bead and star charm to the small end of the shell. To hang, thread a head pin through the hole in the charm, then bend the pin to form a hook. Hang the cherubs from branches painted ivory. Allow some of the branch to be exposed for a shabby chic look.

angels we have heard on high

Rejoicing at our Savior's birth, these heavenly beings shine with glory.

glad tidings

Draped in gold, this gilded angel dons a cording gown, snowflake wings, and a napkin-ring halo.

What You'll Need...

- [ ] 9-inch high cardboard cone
- [ ] 3 yards of gold cording
- [ ] hot-glue gun and glue sticks
- [ ] scissors
- [ ] 1-inch wood doll head
- [ ] gold acrylic paint
- [ ] paintbrush
- [ ] 2 gold-glittered snowflakes
- [ ] napkin ring with gold berries
- [ ] 1-foot length of 1-inch-wide metallic gold ribbon

1 Working with short sections at a time, wrap the cording around the cardboard cone, using hot glue to adhere in place. Cut off excess cording.

2 Paint the wood doll head gold; let it dry.

3 Hot-glue the doll head to the top of the cone. Hot-glue the snowflake wings and napkin-ring halo in place.

4 Tie a bow and hot-glue to the front of the gown.

color burst

Holiday trims cheerfully pop from a winter-white background. Carry the color scheme throughout the room with carefully chosen decorations.

minty fresh

Revive the soft green of yesteryear by pairing the pastel with vivid pinks and reds.

understated elegance

A traditional stocking shape makes a bold statement sewn from floral and paisley in fresh pinks, reds, and green.

What You'll Need...

- waxed paper
- tracing paper
- pencil
- scissors
- ½ yard fabric
- ½ yard contrasting lining fabric
- matching thread
- cording
- sewing needle

1 For each stocking, trace the stocking pattern on page 158; cut out. Use the pattern to cut the stocking front and back and two lining pieces.

2 With right sides facing, sew the stocking front to back; turn. Sew lining pieces together.

3 Slip the lining into the stocking; fold down cuff ¼ inch twice; topstitch.

4 Handstitch a cord end to each stocking top. Tie ribbon bows around the cording.

flirty skirt

Add class to your tree by using refreshing decorator fabric for the skirt. Cut donut shapes in the desired sizes from the fabric and lining, making a single slit through the layers. Align the shapes and zigzag stitch the inner circle and slit. Sew ruffle trim around the outer edge for a polished look.

pretty place setting

Marry mismatched mint green and white dishes for visual interest. Back the place setting with pretty scrapbook papers taped together to make rectangular place mats. To make them wipeable, laminate the mats at a copy shop or office supply store.

70

natural beauty

Blanket a plain canvas with color and simple paint strokes to create a gentle wintry scene.

What You'll Need...

- 18x24-inch wrapped artists's canvas
- acrylic paint in mint green, red, bright pink, and white
- paintbrushes
- tracing paper
- pencil
- transfer paper
- pencil with unused eraser
- clear acrylic spray

1 Paint the entire canvas mint green; let dry.

2 Enlarge and trace the patterns on page 158. Use transfer paper to trace the patterns onto the canvas front and edges.

3 Paint the branches and holly pink. Paint the cardinal red. Dip the pencil eraser in red paint and dot it along the branches as shown on pattern. Dip a clean pencil eraser in white and dot the background to resemble snow.

4 Using a small paintbrush, brush the sides of banches and leaves with white; sprinkle with glitter while wet. Let dry.

5 In a well-ventilated work area, cover work surface with newspaper. Spray the painting with clear acrylic spray. Let dry. Apply a second coat if desired; let dry.

little lady

～ Beaming with personality, these snow gals dressed up with fancy pill box hats look charming.

What You'll Need...

- [ ] white glittered plastic ornaments
- [ ] round papier mâché box bottoms to fit ornaments
- [ ] decorative paper
- [ ] pencil
- [ ] scissors
- [ ] hot-glue gun and glue sticks
- [ ] glue stick
- [ ] trims
- [ ] 14-inch lengths of narrow cord
- [ ] fuzzy pink pom-poms
- [ ] mini pom-poms in black and red
- [ ] ice pick

1 For each ornament, trace box bottom and side onto paper; cut out. Use glue stick to adhere papers to box bottom.

2 Use an ice pick to poke two holes in the center of the box bottom, approximately ¼ inch apart. From the outside, thread a cord end through one of the holes, through the ornament hanger, and back through the remaining hole. With cord ends even, knot them on top of the hat; knot cords close to ends.

3 Hot-glue trims as desired to embellish hat. Hot-glue mini pom-poms in place to make snow gal's face.

72

a flake of a different color

A filigree wood snowflake transforms into a tree topper. Paint it with acrylic paint and sprinkle with glitter. When dry, wire it to the treetop.

jingle bell

A coat of bright pink paint gives a precut wood bell a punch of color. While wet, sprinkle the trim with glitter. Hot-glue a coordinating jingle bell clapper.

perfect match

Choose that "just right" shade of mint to launch your tree trimming. Remove the topper from a clear glass ornament and swirl the paint color in it until the entire inside is coated. Let the paint dry and replace the topper. Tie it with a matching bow.

icy hot

Bright flowers, twigs, and berries suspended in sparkling ice make naturally beautiful luminarias.

74

holly basket

🌿 Encase holly sprigs and pyracantha berries in ice that you mold in a flexible plastic ice cream bucket. Create a candleholder in the center of the ice with a recycled 2-liter bottle. Branches, berries, and water fill the gap between the two containers. Give it a traditional look by placing a red pillar candle in the center and set the finished arrangement in a wire basket.

berry bright

🌿 Make a glowing parfait by alternating layers of cranberries and ice. Use a 2-liter bottle for the outside of the mold and create a hollow place for the candle with a 1-liter bottle. Add a few inches of water and drop a line of cranberries into the gap between the two bottles. Freeze one layer solid, then add more water and berries in the gap and freeze again. Then add a final layer and freeze one last time. Unmold and place a candle in the center.

blazing petals

🌿 Light up the night with a glowing poinsettia encased in ice. Start with small bracts clipped off at the base. Seal the stem with a flame and push the bract face-down into a large plastic cup. Pour distilled water—it makes the clearest ice—into the cup to fill it one-third full. Place a smaller container in the center, weighted with rocks, to create a hollow center in the mold. Freeze until solid. Thaw the ice slightly to unmold both containers. Place a votive candle inside.

winter wonder

A frozen ring of red-twig dogwood, evergreen cuttings, and cranberries warmly embraces a pillar candle. The tall glass holder lets the candle burn brightly —and safely—amid the branches. A flexible plastic cake carrier was used to mold this arrangement.

frozen fruit

Using a flexible plastic container, such as a cut-off recycled 2-liter bottle, is an inexpensive and unbreakable mold for making ice luminarias. Use the same freezing method as for the Blazing Petals, page 75 and below right, arranging branches of yellow-twig dogwood and cranberries in the water.

polka-dot tree

A classic feather tabletop tree enhances the light and festive ambience. Wrap the base in a coordinating towel and nest white balls inside.

carried away

〜 Color coordination is key to this festive basket. Marry similarly wrapped gifts with ornaments in the same hues.

red and white

Striking and traditional, red and white team up to make a cheerful decorating scheme. Paired with simple-to-do projects, the minimalistic outcome is as easy as it is timeless.

not-too-big sprig

❧ The red-and-white theme continues at each place setting, where linen napkins top bistro-style plates. A sprig of rosemary adds an aromatic touch.

beautiful bouquet

❧ Cut stems of crimson amaryllis create a superb Christmasy fresh floral arrangement. Prop stems in a clear glass vase so the lovely blooms get the attention they so deserve.

green to envy

❧ Festooned with contrasting ribbon, a pair of rosemary topiaries makes a delightfully simple centerpiece on the white French linen table runner.

all set for santa

A trio of stockings made from curtain fabric—classic French toile, ticking, and matelassé—brings cheery color to the mantel. Stocking patterns in any simple shape bode well for these no-fuss surprise holders. Complete the environment with a few carefully placed elements, such as a footed bowl of fruit and candles.

ribbon trees

Wrap plastic cones with gingham ribbon and top them with toile bows secured with T-pins. Plant the beribboned trees in terra-cotta pots painted with bright white rims.

fine print

Use a computer and printer as a wrapping paper factory. A repetitive holiday phrase in a script font becomes elegant packaging for small gifts.

party mode

Mismatched place settings in bright punchy colors pop on a sea of silver. To enhance the leaf theme, paint pressed leaves metallic. Scatter the colorful shapes across the table. Alarm clocks set to go off at midnight add to the party mode.

turning over a new leaf

With the flipping of the last page on the calendar comes an influx of New Year's resolutions. Salute this tradition of "turning over a new leaf" with table decorations that are as fitting as they are festive.

vivid invitations

Launch this year's party theme with leaf-laden invitations. Mount the party information on adhesive glitter paper and adhere it to colorful scrapbook paper. Top off the invitation with a shiny metallic leaf.

personalized with pizzazz

Bring the papers used on the invitations to the table as place cards. Place them directly on plates so they stand out among the table decorations.

Join us in honoring our "turning over a new leaf" New Year's resolution: Spending more time with good friends!

What: Pizza & Charades
When: New Year's Eve
Time: 7pm
Where: 707 E. 7th Street

Paul

Napkin Trees

A photo holder does double duty as a napkin stand and place card. Use initial charms found in scrapbooking stores to label each base. Fold each napkin in a triangle before slipping it into the wire spiral.

In a Twinkling
rings and things

◀ Buckle Up

For a classy napkin tie, choose a belt buckle that coordinates with the colors and style of your tablescape. Cross wide ribbon through the center to hold the detail in place.

▼ Bling Ring

Adhere a sparkly dimensional scrapbook sticker to a silver napkin ring for eye-catching wow. Change the look seasonally by swapping out the sticker.

Flowery Favors
Decorate ball ornaments using crafts glue and glitter or adhesive glitter paper. Glue the finished pieces to mirrors, remove the hangers, add water, and insert bouquets.

Perfect Poppers
Surprise guests with small gifts tucked into a cardboard tube laden with pretty papers. Personalize the poppers with printed names inserted into photo charms.

Jingle Ring
Crafts wire threads easily through jingle bells to make napkin rings in a jiffy. Alternating bell sizes and colors results in a pretty pattern.

SAVOR *the* SEASON

Cherish the traditions of making foods that smell marvelous and taste wonderful with menus for a sit-down feast, an open house buffet, and a family brunch—plus recipes for bite-size desserts and soothing drinks.

feast with flair

Bring everyone together to celebrate the season with an elegant sit-down dinner that promises comfort and joy.

Pistachio-and-Peppercorn-Coated Herbed Goat Cheese Balls

Pink peppercorns, no relative of the familiar black variety, are the dried berries of an East India plant. Their pungent, slightly sweet flavor is a good match for goat cheese.

- ⅓ cup roasted salted pistachio nuts, finely chopped
- 1 tablespoon crushed dried pink peppercorns
- ½ of a 10.5- to 11-ounce log fresh mild semisoft goat cheese (chèvre)
- 2 teaspoons finely chopped fresh rosemary
- 1 tablespoon extra virgin olive oil
- 32 small sprigs fresh rosemary

In a small bowl combine nuts and peppercorns; set aside. In a medium bowl use a fork to combine cheese, chopped rosemary, and oil; cover and chill for 15 minutes.

With the palms of your hands, roll teaspoonfuls of cheese mixture into 32 balls. Roll balls in pistachio mixture until coated well. Press a rosemary sprig into the top of each ball and arrange balls in a single layer on a serving tray. Cover and chill at least 15 minutes before serving. Makes 8 servings.

MAKE-AHEAD TIP: Place cheese balls in an airtight container and chill up to 24 hours.

Pistachio-and-Peppercorn-Coated Herbed Goat Cheese Balls

Christmas Sparklers recipe on page 94

*Spice-Rubbed Ham
with Apple-Maple Sauce
recipe on page 94*

93

Christmas Sparklers

You'll find bottled pomegranate juice in the juice section of large supermarkets. It has a beautiful ruby color and tart-sweet flavor. Pictured on page 92.

Pomegranate juice (optional)
Colored and/or coarse
    granulated sugar (optional)
4 cups pomegranate juice, chilled
1 750-ml bottle Prosecco or other
    dry sparkling wine, chilled

To sugar the champagne flute rims, if desired, place pomegranate juice and sugar in separate shallow dishes. Dip the rims of 8 champagne flutes in pomegranate juice, then in sugar to coat.

Pour ½ cup pomegranate juice into each champagne flute; top with about ⅓ cup Prosecco. Makes 8 servings.

Spice-Rubbed Ham with Apple-Maple Sauce

The assertive flavors of garlic, cumin, mustard, and maple blend harmoniously in this delicious holiday entrée. Pictured on page 93.

3 tablespoons packed brown sugar
8 cloves garlic, minced
1 tablespoon ground cumin
1 6- to 8-pound cooked ham
    (shank portion)
½ cup Dijon mustard
¼ cup apple cider
¼ cup pure maple syrup
    Salt
    Black pepper

Preheat oven to 325°F. Combine brown sugar, garlic, and cumin. Score ham by making diagonal cuts in a diamond pattern. Sprinkle ham evenly with sugar mixture; rub in with your fingers. Place ham on a rack in a shallow roasting pan. Insert a meat thermometer into center of ham. The thermometer should not touch bone.

Bake for 1½ to 2¼ hours or until thermometer registers 140°F. Cover loosely with foil the last 30 minutes of cooking to avoid overbrowning.

For sauce, stir together mustard, cider, and maple syrup. Season to taste with salt and pepper. Pass sauce with ham. Makes 10 servings.

Honey-Nut Cheesecake

The flaky phyllo crust, nuts, and honey will remind your taste buds of baklava. Mascarpone, an extra-rich Italian cream cheese, makes the texture sublimely creamy. Pictured opposite.

½ cup ground walnuts, hazelnuts,
    or pecans*
2 tablespoons granulated sugar
12 sheets frozen phyllo dough
    (14×9-inch rectangles), thawed
½ cup butter, melted
2 8-ounce packages cream cheese,
    softened
1 8-ounce container mascarpone
    cheese, softened
⅔ cup honey
2 tablespoons all-purpose flour
¼ cup milk
3 eggs, lightly beaten
2 teaspoons finely shredded
    lemon peel
    Fresh raspberries (optional)
    Fresh rosemary sprig (optional)
    Light-color corn syrup (optional)
    Sanding sugar (optional)

Preheat oven to 325°F. Generously grease the bottom and sides of an 8-inch springform pan. Set aside. In a small bowl combine ground nuts and 2 tablespoons sugar; set aside.

Unfold phyllo dough; remove 1 sheet. (While you work, cover the remaining phyllo dough with plastic wrap to prevent it from drying out.)

Brush dough with some of the melted butter. Place another sheet of phyllo on the first, rotating it slightly to stagger the corners. Brush with a little more of the melted butter. Repeat with remaining phyllo sheets and butter.

Ease the phyllo stack into the prepared pan, pleating it as necessary and being careful not to tear the phyllo. (Let excess phyllo hang over sides of pan.) Sprinkle nut mixture on phyllo in pan.

For filling, in a large mixing bowl combine cream cheese, mascarpone cheese, honey, and flour. Beat with an electric mixer on low speed until smooth. Beat in milk. Using a wooden spoon, stir in eggs and lemon peel.

Pour filling into phyllo crust. Place springform pan in a shallow baking pan. Bake for 50 to 60 minutes or until center appears set when gently shaken.

Cool in springform pan on a wire rack for 1 hour. Using a small thin knife, loosen crust from side of pan. Remove side of pan. Cool for 1 hour more. Cover and chill for at least 6 hours or up to 24 hours. If desired, brush raspberries and rosemary sprig with corn syrup and sprinkle with sanding sugar. Arrange raspberries and rosemary on the cheesecake. Makes 12 servings.

*NOTE: Use a grinder, blender, or food processor to grind the nuts, watching carefully because nuts can form a paste if ground too much.

Honey-Nut Cheesecake

Wild Rice Rosettes

*Wild rice brings irresistible nuttiness to
these parsley-flecked morsels.*

3¾ to 4¼ cups all-purpose flour
2 packages active dry yeast
1 tablespoon snipped fresh parsley
  or 1 teaspoon dried parsley
  flakes, crushed
¾ cup cooked wild rice,* cooled
1¼ cups water
3 tablespoons butter
2 tablespoons sugar
1 teaspoon instant chicken bouillon
  granules
¾ teaspoon salt
2 tablespoons milk
  Butter, melted

In a large mixing bowl stir
together 1½ cups of the flour, the
yeast, and parsley. Stir in cooked rice;
set aside.

In a medium saucepan combine
water, 3 tablespoons butter, sugar,
bouillon granules, and salt. Heat and
stir just until warm (120°F to 130°F),
the butter almost melts, and the
bouillon dissolves. Add water mixture
to flour mixture. Beat with an electric
mixer on low speed for 30 seconds,
scraping bowl constantly. Beat on
high speed for 3 minutes. Using a
wooden spoon, stir in as much of the
remaining flour as you can.

Turn dough out onto a lightly
floured surface. Knead in enough
of the remaining flour to make a
moderately stiff dough that is smooth
and elastic (6 to 8 minutes total).
Shape into a ball. Place in a large
lightly greased bowl; turn once to
grease surface of dough. Cover; let
rise in a warm place until double in
size (45 to 60 minutes).

Punch dough down. Turn out
onto a lightly floured surface. Divide
dough in half. Cover; let rest for
10 minutes. Meanwhile, lightly
grease baking sheets; set aside.

To shape rosettes, roll each dough
half into a 12×10-inch rectangle. Cut
each rectangle crosswise into twelve
10×1-inch strips. Stretch each strip
to 12 inches in length; tie in a loose
knot, leaving two long ends. Tuck top
end under roll; bring up bottom end
and tuck it into center of roll. Place
on prepared baking sheets. Cover and
let rise in a warm place until almost
double in size (about 30 minutes).

Preheat oven to 375°F. Brush
rosettes with milk. Bake for 12 to
15 minutes or until golden brown.
Remove from oven; brush tops with
melted butter. Serve warm. Makes
24 rolls.

***NOTE:** To prepare ¾ cup cooked
wild rice, rinse ¼ cup wild rice well.
In a small saucepan combine wild
rice and 1 cup water. Bring to boiling;
reduce heat. Cover and simmer about
40 minutes or until most of the water
is absorbed. Drain, if necessary.

96

Wild Rice Rosettes

Roasted Brussels Sprouts and Red Onions

Shiitake-Topped Mashed Potatoes

Roasted Brussels Sprouts and Red Onions

If you have sufficient oven space available, you can roast the Brussels sprouts and onions and serve them at once, skipping the chilling step.

2½ pounds Brussels sprouts, trimmed and halved lengthwise
2 medium red onions, cut into thin wedges
2 tablespoons olive oil
½ teaspoon caraway seeds
2 tablespoons cider vinegar

Preheat oven to 400°F. In a large shallow roasting pan toss together sprouts, onions, oil, and caraway seeds. Roast, uncovered, 40 minutes or until sprouts are tender and start to brown, stirring twice.

Transfer sprouts mixture to a large bowl. Cover and chill for up to 24 hours. Place sprouts mixture in a 12-inch skillet. Cook over medium heat until heated through, stirring occasionally. Transfer to a large serving bowl. Sprinkle with vinegar, ½ teaspoon *salt*, and ¼ teaspoon *black pepper*. Toss gently to coat. Makes 8 servings.

Shiitake-Topped Mashed Potatoes

When plain mashed potatoes just won't do, dress up herb-seasoned potatoes with chunky mushroom gravy.

4 to 5 medium russet potatoes (2 pounds)
⅓ to ⅔ cup half-and-half or whole milk
¼ cup butter
¼ cup plain yogurt
½ teaspoon salt
¼ teaspoon black pepper
¾ cup thinly sliced green onions or ⅓ cup snipped fresh chives
3 tablespoons butter
¼ cup finely chopped onion
2 cloves garlic, minced
1 pound fresh shiitake mushrooms, stemmed and sliced
⅓ cup beef broth
⅓ cup Madeira or beef broth
2 tablespoons snipped fresh tarragon
¼ teaspoon salt
¼ teaspoon black pepper
2 tablespoons whipping cream

Peel and quarter potatoes. In a large covered saucepan cook potatoes in enough lightly salted boiling water to cover for 20 to 25 minutes or until tender; drain.

Mash with a potato masher or ricer, or beat with an electric mixer on low speed. Add ⅓ cup of the half-and-half and the ¼ cup butter, stirring potato mixture until nearly smooth. Stir in yogurt, the ½ teaspoon salt, and ¼ teaspoon pepper. If necessary, gradually mash in or beat in enough of the remaining ⅓ cup half-and-half to make mixture light and fluffy. Stir in green onions.

For mushroom gravy, in a medium saucepan heat the 3 tablespoons butter over medium heat. Add onion and garlic; cook and stir for 1 minute. Add mushrooms; cook just until mushrooms are tender, stirring occasionally. Stir in broth, Madeira, tarragon, ¼ teaspoon salt, and ¼ teaspoon pepper. Cook about 3 minutes or until mushrooms are tender, stirring occasionally. Stir in whipping cream. Simmer, uncovered, for 2 minutes more.

To serve, spoon mashed potatoes into a serving bowl. Make a depression in the center; spoon mushroom gravy over potatoes. Makes 8 servings.

Holiday Crostini
recipe on page 100

an open house buffet

Roasted Curried Cashews
recipe on page 100

Welcome guests to your home and get the party started with a crowd-pleasing assortment of appetizers presented in festive ways.

Holiday Crostini

Crostini is a fancy name for baguette slices that have been brushed with oil and baked until golden brown. A creamy ham and Brie topper makes these irresistible. Pictured on page 98.

1 16-ounce loaf baguette-style French bread
Olive oil
1 4½- to 5-ounce round Brie cheese
1½ cups chopped, seeded plum tomatoes
1 cup finely chopped cooked ham (about 6 ounces)
2 tablespoons olive oil
2 tablespoons white balsamic vinegar
1 teaspoon dried oregano, crushed
2 cloves garlic, minced
½ cup finely shredded Italian cheese blend (2 ounces)
Snipped basil (optional)

Preheat oven to 425°F. For crostini, cut French bread into ½-inch-thick slices. Lightly brush both sides of each bread slice with olive oil. Place slices on an ungreased baking sheet. Bake for 5 to 7 minutes or until crisp and light brown, turning once.

Meanwhile, use a vegetable peeler to remove edible rind from Brie cheese. Finely cube cheese. In a medium bowl combine Brie, tomatoes, ham, 2 tablespoons oil, vinegar, oregano, and garlic. Toss to combine. Spoon mixture onto bread slices. Sprinkle with Italian cheese blend. Bake 6 to 8 minutes or until heated through. If desired, garnish with basil. Makes about 30 servings.

TO MAKE AHEAD: Slice and bake bread as directed. Store in a large resealable plastic bag up to 24 hours.

Roasted Curried Cashews

Sweet, salty, and spicy cashews add delightful crunch to the party buffet. Chop up leftover nuts and sprinkle on soups or salads. Pictured on page 99.

3 cups raw cashews (about 1 pound)
3 tablespoons packed brown sugar
2 teaspoons kosher salt
2 teaspoons curry powder
½ teaspoon ground cumin
¼ teaspoon cayenne pepper
¼ cup water
1 tablespoon butter

Preheat oven to 350°F. Line a 15×10×1-inch baking pan with parchment paper or foil. Spread cashews in an even layer in the prepared baking pan. Bake about 10 minutes or until lightly browned.

Meanwhile, in a small bowl combine 2 tablespoons of the brown sugar, the salt, curry powder, cumin, and cayenne pepper; set aside.

In a large saucepan combine water, butter, and the remaining 1 tablespoon brown sugar. Bring to boiling, stirring constantly. Add cashews, stirring to coat. Cook and stir about 2 minutes or until liquid evaporates. Remove from heat. Add curry mixture; toss gently to coat.

Spread nuts in an even layer in the same baking pan. Bake for 12 to 15 minutes or until golden brown, stirring once. Cool in pan on a wire rack. Makes 14 (¼-cup) servings.

TO MAKE AHEAD: Store roasted cashews in an airtight container or resealable plastic bag at room temperature up to 1 week.

Marinated Shrimp Scampi

Marinate the shrimp briefly in a lemony wine marinade and broil just before party guests arrive. Sweet pepper and parsley add holiday flair. Pictured opposite.

2 pounds fresh or frozen extra-jumbo shrimp in shells (30 to 40)
¼ cup olive oil
¼ cup dry white wine
6 cloves garlic, minced
2 teaspoons finely shredded lemon peel
½ teaspoon salt
½ teaspoon crushed red pepper
2 tablespoons chopped red sweet pepper
2 tablespoons fresh snipped parsley
Lemon wedges

Thaw shrimp, if frozen. Peel and devein shrimp, leaving tails intact. Rinse shrimp and pat dry with paper towels. Place shrimp in a resealable plastic bag set in a shallow bowl.

For marinade, in a small bowl combine olive oil, wine, garlic, lemon peel, salt, and crushed red pepper. Pour over shrimp. Seal bag and toss gently to coat shrimp. Marinate in the refrigerator for 1 hour.

Preheat broiler. Remove shrimp from marinade, reserving marinade. Arrange shrimp on unheated broiler pan. Broil 4 to 5 inches from heat for 2 minutes. Turn shrimp over and brush with reserved marinade; broil 2 to 4 minutes more or until shrimp are opaque. Discard any remaining marinade. Makes 10 to 12 servings.

To serve, mound shrimp on a serving platter and sprinkle with sweet pepper and parsley. Serve with lemon wedges.

Time-Savvy Tips

Complete some of the prep for this succulent shrimp appetizer the day before your party.
■ Prepare the marinade. Cover and store in the refrigerator up to 24 hours.
■ If the shrimp you purchase are frozen, place them in a sealed container and thaw overnight in the refrigerator.
■ Peel and devein fresh shrimp and refrigerate in a covered container.

Buying Shrimp

■ The price of shrimp usually depends on the size—the bigger the shrimp, the higher the price and the fewer per pound.
■ Look for firm, juicy shrimp with translucent, moist shells and without black spots (unless you purchase black tiger shrimp).

101

Marinated Shrimp Scampi

Blue Cheese-Walnut Spread

Blue Cheese-Walnut Spread

Prepare and refrigerate this tasty spread up to 2 days before your party. Let it stand at room temperature for 1 hour. Stir the mixture well to soften, then garnish and serve. Pictured opposite.

2 4-ounce packages (2 cups) crumbled blue cheese
½ cup unsalted butter, softened*
½ cup finely chopped walnuts, toasted
Coarsely chopped walnuts, toasted (optional)
Snipped chives (optional)
Flatbread and/or apple slices

In a food processor combine crumbled blue cheese and butter. Cover and process until nearly smooth, scraping down sides of bowl as needed. Stir in the ½ cup walnuts. Transfer to a small serving bowl.

If desired, sprinkle with coarsely chopped walnuts and chives. Serve with flatbread and/or apple slices. Makes 16 (2-tablespoon) servings.

*NOTE: To quickly soften a stick of butter, heat it, unwrapped, in the microwave oven on 50 percent power (medium) at 10-second intervals.

Parmesan Cheese Straws

Parmesan Cheese Straws

These cheese-filled pastry strips can be made ahead and frozen up to 1 month.

½ cup grated Parmigiano-Reggiano cheese (2 ounces)
½ teaspoon dried basil, crushed
¼ teaspoon garlic powder
1 sheet frozen puff pastry (½ of a 17.3-ounce package), thawed
1 egg

Preheat oven to 400°F. In a small bowl combine cheese, basil, and garlic powder. Set aside.

On a lightly floured surface roll thawed pastry sheet into a 14×12-inch rectangle. Cut the rectangle in half crosswise to form two 12×7-inch rectangles.

In a small bowl whisk together egg and 1 tablespoon water. Lightly brush both pastry rectangles with some of the egg mixture.

Sprinkle cheese mixture on one of the rectangles. Top with the other rectangle, brushed side down. Using your fingers, firmly press rectangles together, forcing out air pockets and sealing the edges. Brush pastry top with egg mixture.

Using a pastry wheel or sharp knife, cut pastry crosswise into ½-inch-wide strips. Arrange strips 1 inch apart on ungreased baking sheets. Holding both ends, twist each pastry strip, pressing ends into the baking sheet to secure. Bake for 9 to 11 minutes or until straws are golden and crisp. Cool slightly before removing from the baking sheet. Makes 24 straws.

Sweet, Hot, and Sour Meatballs

Wrap-and-Roll Basil Pinwheels

104

Wrap-and-Roll Basil Pinwheels

Colorful tortillas and purchased cheese spread add flair to these popular make-ahead party bites. They're also a tasty addition on holiday soup buffets.

- 3 7- or 8-inch flour tortillas
- 1 5.2-ounce container semisoft cheese with garlic and herbs (such as Boursin brand)
- 12 large fresh basil leaves
- ½ of a 7-ounce jar roasted red sweet peppers, drained and cut into ¼-inch strips
- 4 ounces thinly sliced cooked ham, roast beef, or turkey
  Snipped fresh basil (optional)

Spread tortillas evenly with cheese (if cheese seems crumbly, stir it until smooth). Cover cheese with large basil leaves; arrange roasted peppers on basil. Top with meat.

Tightly roll up each tortilla; wrap in plastic wrap. Chill tortilla rolls for 2 to 4 hours.

To serve, trim ends of rolls; cut rolls into 1-inch slices. If desired, secure each slice with a short skewer and garnish with snipped fresh basil. Makes 18 to 20 servings.

Sweet, Hot, and Sour Meatballs

Keep these zippy meatballs warm in a chafing dish or in a slow cooker on warm or low-heat setting up to 2 hours.

- 1 16-ounce package (32) frozen cooked plain meatballs
- ⅓ cup apple jelly
- 3 tablespoons spicy brown mustard
- 3 tablespoons apple juice
- ½ teaspoon Worcestershire sauce
  Few dashes bottled hot pepper sauce

Preheat oven to 350°F. Place frozen meatballs in single layer in a shallow baking pan. Bake about 20 minutes or until heated through.

Meanwhile, in a large saucepan stir together jelly, mustard, apple juice, Worcestershire sauce, and hot pepper sauce. Cook and stir over medium heat until bubbly.

Use a slotted spoon to transfer meatballs to jelly mixture; stir gently to coat. Return to boiling; reduce heat. Simmer for 3 to 5 minutes or until sauce thickens, stirring occasionally. Serve meatballs with short skewers. Makes 10 servings.

Fennel and Onion Dip

Offer this flavorful dip with sweet pepper wedges, sugar snap peas, and cucumber slices. Pictured opposite.

- 1 medium fennel bulb
- 1 16-ounce container sour cream French onion-flavor dip
- 2 tablespoons finely chopped red onion
- 2 tablespoons thinly sliced green onion (1 medium)
  Red onion slivers (optional)
  Assorted vegetable dippers

Trim feathery leaves from fennel; discard. Trim fennel bulb. Chop enough of the bulb to measure 1 cup.

In a medium bowl combine the chopped fennel, onion dip, chopped red onion, and green onion.

Transfer dip to a serving bowl. If desired, garnish with red onion slivers. Serve with vegetable dippers. Makes 18 (2-tablespoon) servings.

TO MAKE AHEAD: Prepare dip and transfer to serving bowl as directed. Cover and chill up to 24 hours. Prepare assorted vegetable dippers and chill separately. Serve as directed.

Fennel and Onion Dip

Prosciutto with
Asparagus and New Potatoes

a festive brunch

There's no time like the holidays to host a houseful of overnight guests. Dish up a midmorning meal of breakfast specials that offers last-minute or make-ahead ease.

Prosciutto with Asparagus and New Potatoes

Elegant ribbons of Parmesan cheese make this an eye- and palate-pleasing salad for brunch. To make the ribbons, use a swivel-blade vegetable peeler to shave thin slices from a solid piece of cheese.

1½ pounds fresh asparagus spears
1 20-ounce package refrigerated new potato wedges
¼ cup bottled Italian salad dressing
1 teaspoon finely shredded lemon peel
6 ounces thinly sliced prosciutto slices
Parmesan cheese ribbons (optional)

Snap off and discard woody bases from the asparagus spears. If desired, scrape off scales. Cut into 2-inch pieces. Set aside.

In a large saucepan cook the potatoes, covered, in a small amount of lightly salted boiling water for 11 minutes.

Add asparagus. Cook, covered, about 4 minutes more or until asparagus is crisp-tender and potatoes are tender; drain. Transfer to a serving platter.

Meanwhile, in a small bowl combine salad dressing and lemon peel. Drizzle salad dressing mixture over potatoes and asparagus.

Arrange prosciutto slices beside vegetables. If desired, top with Parmesan cheese ribbons. Serve warm. Makes 8 servings.

Apple Butter Hot Cakes

Make the honey- and cinnamon-flavored butter and luscious cherry sauce ahead so you can set the butter out and warm the sauce while cooking the mini-size hot cakes.

½ cup butter, softened
¼ cup honey
¼ teaspoon ground cinnamon
1 12-ounce package frozen pitted light or dark sweet cherries
½ cup cherry jam or cherry preserves
1 teaspoon finely shredded orange peel
1½ cups packaged regular or buttermilk pancake mix (not complete pancake mix)
¾ cup milk
2 tablespoons cooking oil
2 eggs, lightly beaten
½ cup purchased apple butter

For honey-flavored butter, in a small bowl whisk together softened butter, honey, and cinnamon. Set aside.

For cherry sauce, in a saucepan combine frozen cherries, cherry jam, and orange peel. Bring to boiling over medium heat, stirring frequently; reduce heat. Simmer, uncovered, for 10 minutes or until sauce thickens. Cover and set aside; keep warm.

In a medium bowl stir together pancake mix, milk, cooking oil, eggs, and apple butter. Stir just until moistened (batter will be lumpy). For mini-size hot cakes, spread about 1 tablespoon batter into a 1½-inch circle onto a hot lightly greased griddle or heavy skillet. (For standard-size hot cakes, spread about ¼ cup batter into a 4-inch circle.) Cook over medium heat about 2 minutes on each side or until hot cakes are golden, turning when hot cakes have bubbly surfaces and edges are slightly dry.

Serve warm with flavored butter and cherry sauce. Makes 32 to 40 mini or 8 to 10 standard hot cakes.

Mocha au Lait

Looking for an easy and impressive last-minute gift? Package one or more batches of this coffee- and chocolate-flavored drink mix in clear cellophane bags and tie with festive ribbons. Include instructions so your java-loving friends can whip up a great mocha sensation.

¾ cup instant creamer
⅓ cup packed brown sugar
½ cup instant coffee crystals
⅔ cup miniature semisweet chocolate pieces
Shaved semisweet chocolate (optional)

In a medium bowl combine creamer, brown sugar, coffee crystals, and chocolate pieces. Store mixture in a tightly covered container. Makes 2 cups mix (enough for 8 servings).

For each serving, pour ⅔ cup hot water in a blender container. Add ¼ cup of the mix. Cover tightly; blend until well combined and frothy. (Or beat with a wire whisk or electric mixer.) Pour into a mug. If desired, top with shaved chocolate.

109

Individual Ham and Cheese Quiches

It's so easy. Start with purchased piecrusts; bake and fill with a tasty ham and egg mixture. This recipe can also be made in a 10-inch tart pan. See directions below. Pictured opposite.

Cranberry Ice

1 15-ounce package rolled refrigerated unbaked piecrust (2 crusts)
½ cup shredded Italian cheese blend
½ cup finely chopped red sweet pepper
¼ cup finely chopped peppered or smoked cooked ham
1 tablespoon thinly sliced green onion or 1½ teaspoons snipped fresh chives
1½ teaspoons all-purpose flour
¼ teaspoon Italian seasoning, crushed
⅛ teaspoon salt
⅛ teaspoon black pepper
3 eggs, slightly beaten
½ cup half-and-half, light cream, or milk
Fresh herb springs, such as basil, oregano, or thyme (optional)

Let piecrusts stand at room temperature according to package directions. Preheat oven to 400°F.

Cut each piecrust into 4 equal sections (8 sections total). Press sections of piecrust onto the bottom and up the sides of eight 4-inch fluted individual tart pans with removable bottoms. Trim excess dough from tops of pans.

Line each pastry shell with a double thickness of foil. Place pans on a baking sheet. Bake for 7 minutes. Remove foil. Bake for 2 to 3 minutes more or until pastry is set and dry.

Remove pastry shells from oven; set aside. Reduce oven temperature to 325°F.

In a medium bowl combine shredded Italian cheese blend, sweet pepper, ham, green onion, flour, Italian seasoning, salt, and black pepper. Divide mixture evenly among pastry shells.

In the same bowl beat together eggs and half-and-half. Pour egg mixture over filling mixture in each pastry shell. Bake for 20 minutes or until filling is set. Let stand for 5 minutes before serving. If desired, top each with a fresh herb sprig. Makes 8 servings.

To make 1 large quiche: Preheat oven to 400°F. Line a 10-inch tart pan with removable bottom with one piecrust (reserve remaining piecrust for another use). Line picrust with double thickness of foil. Bake for 7 minutes. Remove foil and bake for 8 to 9 minutes more or until pastry is set, dry, and lightly browned. Reduce oven temperature to 325°F. Sprinkle cheese mixture evenly in baked piecrust. Pour egg mixture over cheese. Bake for 30 minutes or until set. Let stand for 10 minutes before serving.

Cranberry Ice

Nothing could be easier than this light and refreshing concoction—just cook and puree the cranberries, strain, and freeze. It's the perfect palate-pleaser to serve between courses at a brunch.

1½ cups water
¾ cup sugar
2 cups cranberries

Line an 8×4×2-inch loaf pan with plastic wrap; set aside. In a saucepan combine water, sugar, and cranberries. Cook over medium heat just until mixture boils, stirring to dissolve sugar. Remove from heat; cool slightly. Pour, half at a time, into a blender or food processor. Cover and blend or process until mixture is nearly smooth. Strain through a fine-mesh sieve (you should have 2 to 2½ cups sieved cranberry mixture).

Pour sieved mixture into lined loaf pan. Cover and freeze for 2 hours or until mixture is nearly frozen. Stir well, scraping frozen mixture from sides of pan. Spread mixture evenly. Cover and freeze overnight.

To serve, let stand at room temperature for 5 to 10 minutes. Spoon into serving dishes. Makes 8 to 10 servings.

petite pleasures

Let luscious mini versions of cakes, cookies, and tarts or frosty dessert drinks provide the sweet decadence that everyone craves at holiday parties and dinners.

Mini Snowball Cakes

Mini Snowball Cakes

Create fun and fancy mini cakes with a cake mix fix-up. Pictured opposite.

Nonstick cooking spray
1 package 1-layer-size white
   cake mix
½ cup canned eggnog
1 egg
1 teaspoon vanilla
⅛ teaspoon ground nutmeg
1 3-ounce package cream cheese,
   softened
2 tablespoons butter, softened
¾ cup powdered sugar
½ teaspoon vanilla
1 to 2 tablespoons milk
¾ cup shredded coconut

Preheat oven to 350°F. Lightly coat thirty-six 1¾-inch muffin cups with cooking spray or line muffin cups with paper bake cups; set aside.

In a medium mixing bowl combine cake mix, eggnog, egg, 1 teaspoon vanilla, and nutmeg. Beat with an electric mixer on low speed just until combined. Beat on medium speed for 2 minutes, scraping sides of bowl. Divide batter evenly among the prepared muffin cups, filling each about two-thirds full (about 1 rounded teaspoon in each).

Bake for 10 to 12 minutes or until a toothpick inserted in the centers comes out clean. Cool in muffin cups on a wire rack for 5 minutes. Remove from muffin cups; cool.

For frosting, in a medium mixing bowl combine cream cheese and butter. Beat with an electric mixer on medium speed until combined. Beat in powdered sugar and ½ teaspoon vanilla. Beat in enough of the milk, 1 teaspoon at a time, to make a frosting of spreading consistency.

Dip tops of mini cakes into frosting, then into coconut. Makes 36 mini cakes.

Glazed Almond Shortbread Stacks

3 tablespoons granulated sugar
2 teaspoons butter, cut up
½ cup sliced almonds, toasted
1¼ cups all-purpose flour
3 tablespoons packed brown
   sugar
½ cup butter
2 tablespoons sliced almonds,
   finely chopped
1 3-ounce package cream
   cheese, softened
4 teaspoons powdered sugar
¼ teaspoon finely shredded
   orange peel
1 teaspoon orange juice

For glazed almonds, line a baking sheet with foil. Lightly butter the foil; set baking sheet aside. Place granulated sugar in a medium heavy skillet. Heat over medium-high heat, shaking skillet several times to heat sugar evenly (do not stir). Heat until some of the sugar melts and looks syrupy. Start to stir only the melted sugar to keep it from overbrowning; stir in the remaining sugar as it melts. Reduce heat to low. Continue to cook and stir until all of the sugar melts and is golden brown. Stir in the 2 teaspoons butter. Add the sliced almonds to skillet, stirring

to coat. Pour nut mixture onto the prepared baking sheet. Using 2 forks, separate nut mixture into small clusters while still warm. Cool.

Preheat oven to 325°F. In a medium bowl combine flour and brown sugar. Using a pastry blender, cut in the ½ cup butter until mixture resembles fine crumbs and starts to cling. Stir in the finely chopped almonds. Knead until smooth and shape into a ball. On a lightly floured surface roll dough to ¼-inch thickness. Using a 1½-inch scalloped round cutter, cut dough. Place cutouts 1 inch apart on ungreased cookie sheet.

Bake about 20 minutes or just until bottoms start to brown and cookies are set. Transfer to a wire rack; cool.

For frosting, in a small mixing bowl combine cream cheese and powdered sugar. Beat with an electric mixer on medium speed until smooth. Add orange peel and orange juice; beat until combined. If necessary, stir in additional orange juice to make a frosting of spreading consistency.

To assemble, spread shortbread rounds with cream cheese frosting; top with glazed almond clusters. Makes about 28 cookies.

*Glazed Almond
Shortbread Stacks*

Raspberry Brownie Tartlets

Raspberry Brownie Tartlets

These exquisite mini-size desserts boast three kinds of chocolate—cocoa powder in the pastry, unsweetened baking chocolate in the brownie layer, and semisweet chocolate in the velvety ganache. They're sure to become a holiday favorite.

1 recipe Chocolate Pastry
1 ounce unsweetened chocolate, chopped
2 tablespoons butter
⅓ cup sugar
¼ cup seedless red raspberry jam
1 egg, lightly beaten
⅓ cup all-purpose flour
¼ teaspoon baking powder
⅛ teaspoon salt
24 red raspberries
1 recipe Chocolate Ganache

Preheat oven to 375°F. On a lightly floured surface roll the Chocolate Pastry to ⅛-inch thickness. Using a 2¾-inch round cookie cutter, cut pastry into 24 rounds. Fit rounds into 24 ungreased 1¾-inch muffin cups, pressing onto bottoms and up sides. Bake for 5 minutes.

Meanwhile, for filling, in a small saucepan combine unsweetened chocolate and butter. Cook and stir over low heat until melted. Remove from heat. Stir in sugar, jam, and egg just until combined. Stir in flour, baking powder, and salt. Spoon a scant 1 tablespoon of the filling into each pastry-lined muffin cup.

Bake for 12 to 15 minutes or until filling is set. Cool in muffin cups on a wire rack for 5 minutes. Remove from muffin cups; cool. Top each tartlet with a raspberry. Spoon Chocolate Ganache over berry. Makes 24 tartlets.

CHOCOLATE PASTRY: In a medium bowl stir together 1¼ cups all-purpose flour, ⅓ cup sugar, and ¼ cup unsweetened cocoa powder. Using a pastry blender, cut in ½ cup cold butter until mixture is crumbly. In a small bowl whisk together 1 egg yolk and 2 tablespoons cold water. Gradually stir egg yolk mixture into flour mixture. Gently knead dough just until a ball forms. If necessary, cover dough with plastic wrap and chill for 30 to 60 minutes or until dough is easy to handle.

CHOCOLATE GANACHE: In a small saucepan heat ¼ cup whipping cream over medium-high heat just until boiling. Remove from heat. Add ½ cup semisweet chocolate pieces (do not stir). Let stand for 5 minutes. Stir mixture until smooth. Cool for 15 minutes before using.

TO MAKE AHEAD: Layer tartlets without berries and ganache between waxed paper in an airtight container; cover. Store at room temperature up to 2 days or freeze up to 1 month. To serve, thaw tartlets if frozen. Finish as directed.

Peppermint Frost

The cool flavor of peppermint gets a creamy twist that goes down easy, thanks to crème de cacao, light cream, and a smattering of candy. Pictured opposite.

1 lemon wedge
2 tablespoons finely crushed peppermint sticks
1 lemon wedge
2 ounces (¼ cup) white crème de cacao
1½ ounces (3 tablespoons) peppermint Schnapps
3 tablespoons half-and-half or light cream
1 ounce (2 tablespoons) vodka
¾ cup ice cubes

Rub rims of eight 1½- to 2-ounce shot glasses with lemon wedge. Dip rims in crushed candy; set aside.

In a blender combine crème de cacao, Schnapps, half-and-half, and vodka. Add ice cubes. Cover; blend until smooth. Pour mixture into prepared glasses. Serve immediately. Makes 8 (1½-ounce) servings.

114

Peppermint Frost

115

Cranberry-Lime
Mousse Cups

Brandy-Kissed Snowflakes

✳

The rich flavor of brandy gets a mellow touch with the addition of whipped cream and white crème de cacao—the perfect end to an evening. Pictured opposite.

¾ cup vanilla ice cream
3 ounces (⅓ cup) brandy
2 ounces (¼ cup) white crème de cacao
½ cup ice cubes
Whipped cream
Ground cinnamon

In a blender combine ice cream, brandy, and crème de cacao. Add ice cubes. Cover and blend until thoroughly blended. Pour mixture into eight 1½- to 2-ounce shot glasses. Top each with whipped cream piped through a star tip. Sprinkle lightly with cinnamon. Serve immediately or nest in ice. Makes 8 (1½-ounce) servings.

Cranberry-Lime Mousse Cups

Dried cranberries lend distinctive flavor to this holiday dessert. The creamy mixture is so rich, you'll want to serve it in small portions.

½ cup sugar
½ of an envelope unflavored gelatin
½ cup frozen cranberry juice concentrate, thawed
1 teaspoon finely shredded lime peel (set aside)
¼ cup fresh lime juice
¼ cup dried cranberries, finely snipped
2 cups whipping cream
Finely shredded lime peel (optional)

In a small saucepan stir together the sugar and unflavored gelatin. Stir in cranberry juice concentrate. Heat over low heat just until sugar and gelatin dissolve. Transfer mixture to a small bowl; cover and chill for 1 hour or until mixture thickens. In another small bowl combine lime juice and cranberries. Let stand for 10 minutes. Do not drain.

In a large chilled mixing bowl beat whipping cream with an electric mixer on medium speed until soft peaks form (tips curl). Gently fold in chilled gelatin mixture, dried cranberry mixture, and 1 teaspoon lime peel. Divide mixture evenly among small shot or cordial glasses. Chill at least 30 minutes or up to 24 hours before serving. If desired, garnish with additional lime peel. Makes 16 servings.

Tiramisu Tippers

✳

½ cup coffee ice cream
1 ounce (2 tablespoons) vodka
1 ounce (2 tablespoons) coffee liqueur
½ ounce (1 tablespoon) crème de cacao
½ cup ice cubes
Chocolate-covered coffee beans, coarsely chopped (optional)

In a blender combine ice cream, vodka, coffee liqueur, and crème de cacao. Add ice. Cover and blend until smooth. Pour mixture into 8 espresso cups. If desired, top each with coffee beans. Serve drinks immediately or nest in ice. Makes 8 (1-ounce) servings.

Brandy-Kissed
Snowflakes

Spiced Christmas Tea ▶

In a medium saucepan bring 2 cups water to boiling. Add 3 unflavored black tea bags, 4 star anise, and 3 inches stick cinnamon; reduce heat. Simmer, uncovered, for 3 to 5 minutes. Remove tea bags and cinnamon sticks; discard. Stir in 1 cup passion fruit nectar or apricot nectar, 3 tablespoons honey, and 2 tablespoons lemon juice. Heat through. Pour tea mixture into 4 heatproof cups. If desired, garnish with cinnamon stick and orange peel twist. Makes 4 (6-ounce) servings.

In a Twinkling
fresh sips

◀ Espresso Cloud with Vanilla

In a medium saucepan stir together 1¼ cups whole milk, 1¼ cups brewed espresso, and ½ cup whipping cream. Heat through over low heat (do not boil). In a medium mixing bowl beat ¼ cup whipping cream, 1 tablespoon powdered sugar, and ½ teaspoon vanilla with an electric mixer until soft peaks form. To serve, pour coffee mixture into mugs; top each with whipped cream. If desired, sprinkle with crushed chocolate-covered espresso beans. Makes 4 (6-ounce) servings.

Pineapple Mimosas ▶

In a large pitcher combine one 12-ounce can frozen pineapple juice concentrate, thawed; one 6-ounce can frozen limeade concentrate, thawed; and 2 cups cold water. Chill thoroughly. Divide mixture among 12 champagne flutes. Top with chilled pink champagne or sparkling apple juice (you'll need 6 cups). If desired, garnish with thin pineapple wedges. Makes 12 servings.

Orange-Spiced Coffee

Place a coffee filter in coffee filter basket of a 10-cup electric drip coffeemaker. Combine ¼ to ⅓ cup ground coffee, ½ teaspoon ground cinnamon, ⅛ teaspoon ground allspice, and ⅛ teaspoon ground cloves in coffee filter. Fill carafe with water. Prepare coffee according to coffeemaker directions. Stir in 2 tablespoons orange liqueur and, if desired, 2 tablespoons packed brown sugar. Serve immediately. Makes 8 (6-ounce) servings.

▲ **White Wine Spritzers**

In a large punch bowl combine one 750-milliliter bottle sweet white wine (such as Pinot Grigio) and ¾ cup white grape juice or apple juice. Just before serving slowly pour in one 1-liter bottle desired flavor low-calorie sparkling water, chilled. If desired, garnish individual servings with skewers of fresh fruit, such as red and green grapes, raspberries, and kiwi slices. Makes 10 (6-ounce) servings.

GIVE *from* the HEART

You're in store for a sleighful of heartfelt thank-yous and feel-good moments when you share presents you make and give with love.

game day

A sign board embellished with a pressed-wood medallion makes a handsome cribbage board.

cribbage board

◆ Choose the just-right medallion to personalize a cribbage board for any card player on your gift list.

What You'll Need...

- [ ] tracing paper
- [ ] pencil
- [ ] scissors
- [ ] 12-inch sign board
- [ ] pressed wood medallions to fit ends of cribbage board
- [ ] painter's tape
- [ ] ice pick or awl
- [ ] electric drill with ⅛-inch bit
- [ ] fine-grit sandpaper
- [ ] tack cloth
- [ ] wood glue
- [ ] clear water-based urethane
- [ ] foam paintbrush
- [ ] ³⁄₁₆-inch dowel
- [ ] electric pencil sharpener or knife

1. Trace the hole pattern on page 158. Trim the paper approximately ½ inch beyond the markings.

2. Center the pattern on the right side of the sign board; tape in place. Use the ice pick to poke holes in the wood at each dot as shown in Photo A. Remove pattern.

3. Using the indentations as guides, drill holes approximately halfway into the depth of the board as shown in Photo B. Lightly sand the board and medallion if needed; wipe away dust with a tack cloth.

4. Glue a medallion to each end of the board; let dry.

5. Brush a coat of urethane onto the top and sides of the board; let dry. Sand lightly and wipe with a tack cloth. Brush on a second coat of urethane and let dry.

6. To make 4 pegs, sharpen one end with a pencil sharpener or whittle with a knife and trim the opposite side to make a 1¼-inch-long peg. Sand any rough edges and wipe with tack cloth. Brush the pegs with a light coat of urethane; let dry.

A

B

123

treasure trove

Crafts stores offer a variety of unfinished wood boxes to personalize for a special jewelry lover of any age.

jewelry box

It's easy to change the box to suit the recipient. Just swap out the embellishments to get the desired look.

What You'll Need...

- wooden box in desired size with framed or flat top
- fine-grit sandpaper
- tack cloth
- newspaper
- acrylic paint in desired colors
- paintbrush
- water-based urethane in desired sheen
- ruler
- decorative scrapbook paper to coordinate with paint
- paper trimmer
- decoupage medium
- beaded sticker to fit approximately half of box lid
- pressed-board initials
- hot-glue gun and glue sticks

1 Lightly sand rough areas on wood box; wipe away dust with a tack cloth.

2 Cover the work surface with newspaper. Paint the box as desired, leaving the top of the lid unpainted; let dry. Coat painted areas with urethane; let dry. Apply a second coat and let dry.

3 Measure the area of the lid that the paper will cover; trim paper to size. Following the manufacturer's directions, use decoupage medium to adhere paper to lid; let dry.

4 Apply beaded sticker to left side of lid. Hot-glue pressed-board initials to lower right side of lid.

cool coil

A nifty wrapped-rope bowl is super simple to machine-sew in any size or color.

coin catcher

 Sew this soft bowl to hold pocket change and keys or fill it with wrapped candies before giving it away.

What You'll Need...

- 5 different fabrics, cut into 45×1-inch-strips (number of strips is determined by how much they are overlapped on the rope)
- 100%-cotton rope, approximately ¼-inch diameter
- sewing needle
- decorative thread for bobbin
- regular sewing thread for top

1 Start bowl at center bottom. Wrap fabric over one end of the rope, slightly overlapping fabric so the rope does not show through. Coil fabric-wrapped rope; hand tack center to start.

2 Continue coiling fabric-wrapped rope, machine-zigzagging to secure the coils together. Add fabric strips, randomly or in a pattern, as necessary. Shape bowl by angling bowl upward while zigzag stitching.

3 When desired shape and size is reached, cut rope, wrap end with fabric, and secure with zigzag stitches. Trim off fabric tail.

Marshmallow-Candy
Bar Fudge

Create delightful handcrafted packages that provide as much enjoyment as the homemade chocolaty goodies they hold.

ultimate chocolate gifts

Marshmallow-Candy Bar Fudge

4½ cups sugar
1 12-ounce can evaporated milk
½ teaspoon salt
1 pound milk chocolate bar, chopped
1 12-ounce package (2 cups) semisweet chocolate pieces
1 7-ounce jar marshmallow crème
1 teaspoon vanilla
  Melted semisweet chocolate
  Whole walnuts

Line a 13×9×2-inch baking pan with foil, extending the foil over the edges of the pan. Butter the foil; set pan aside.

Butter the sides of a heavy 3-quart saucepan. In the saucepan combine sugar, evaporated milk, and salt. Cook and stir over medium-high heat until mixture boils. Reduce heat to medium; continue cooking and stirring for 10 minutes.

Remove saucepan from heat. Add milk chocolate, chocolate pieces, marshmallow crème, and vanilla. Stir until chocolate melts and mixture is combined. Using a wooden spoon, beat by hand for 3 to 5 minutes or until mixture starts to thicken.

Immediately pour fudge into the prepared pan; shake pan gently to spread fudge to edges of pan. Cover; chill for 2 to 3 hours or until firm.

When fudge is firm, use foil to lift it out of pan. Dot the block of fudge with melted semisweet chocolate and top with whole walnuts. Let chocolate set.

Store fudge, tightly covered, at room temperature up to 2 days or in the refrigerator up to 1 month. Makes about 5 pounds (96 pieces).

for the box

With the array of decorative card stock available, you can craft pretty boxes in whatever patterns you like. Enlarge and use the pattern on page 157 to cut the box shape. Follow the fold lines on the pattern to guide folding. A glue stick holds the box sides together. If needed, use paper clips to hold paper pieces in place until the glue dries.

*Bittersweet Chocolate
Pecan Bark*

130

for the plate

Stack contrasting paper plates for a fun,
spirited look. Trim top plate to a smaller size using
decorative-edge scissors. Paper-punch a pair of
holes on one side and thread with coordinating
cord; tie into a bow. Slide a gift tag on cord, knot
both tails, and hot-glue jingle bells on each end.

Bittersweet Chocolate Pecan Bark

For easy drizzling, place the melted candy coating in a heavy resealable plastic bag and snip one of the corners. Pictured opposite.

  2 2-ounce squares vanilla-flavored candy coating, coarsely chopped
  1 11.5-ounce package bittersweet chocolate pieces
  1 cup chopped pecans, toasted

Line a baking sheet with waxed paper; set aside.

Place candy coating in a medium microwave-safe bowl. Microwave, uncovered, on 50% power (medium) for 1 to 2 minutes or until candy coating melts, stirring once halfway through cooking time. Stir mixture until smooth.

Place chocolate pieces in another medium microwave-safe bowl. Microwave, uncovered, on 50% power (medium) for 2 to 3 minutes or until chocolate melts, stirring once. Stir until smooth.

Spread melted chocolate pieces into a 12×9-inch rectangle on prepared baking sheet. Sprinkle evenly with pecans; press lightly into chocolate. Drizzle melted candy coating over top. Chill for 15 minutes or until firm. Peel away the waxed paper. Break into pieces. Makes about 1¼ pounds (about 30 pieces).

TO MAKE AHEAD: Prepare as directed. Layer pieces between waxed paper in an airtight container; cover. Store in the refrigerator up to 1 week. Serve at room temperature.

for the tray

A metal palette is perfect for holding homemade candies and mini ornaments. To trim center, cut two paper circles, one slightly smaller than the other. Punch out snowflakes from the top layer; hold together with glue stick. Use double-sided tape to adhere the medallion in place.

131

Triple-Chocolate Truffles

12 ounces semisweet chocolate, coarsely chopped
 ½ of an 8-ounce package cream cheese, cut up and softened
  4 teaspoons instant coffee crystals
  1 teaspoon water
1⅓ cups milk chocolate pieces or semisweet chocolate pieces
  2 tablespoons shortening
  2 ounces milk chocolate and/or white baking chocolate, coarsely chopped

In a medium heavy saucepan cook and stir semisweet chocolate over low heat. Remove from heat; stir in cream cheese until combined. Stir together coffee crystals and water; add to chocolate mixture and stir until smooth. Cover and chill about 2 hours or until firm.

Line a baking sheet with waxed paper. Use 2 spoons to shape truffle mixture into 1-inch balls; place on prepared baking sheet. Cover; chill for 1 to 2 hours or until firm.

In a medium heavy saucepan cook and stir chocolate pieces and shortening over low heat until melted and smooth. Remove from heat; cool to room temperature.

Use a fork to dip truffles into chocolate mixture, allowing excess chocolate to drip back into saucepan. Return truffles to baking sheet; chill about 30 minutes or until firm.

In a heavy saucepan cook and stir the desired 2 ounces chocolate over low heat until smooth. Drizzle on the truffles. Chill until chocolate sets. Makes 30 truffles.

To store, place truffles in a tightly covered container in the refrigerator. Let stand at room temperature about 30 minutes before serving.

Chocolate-Cherry Cookies

Bright red maraschino cherries wrapped in a chocolaty dough provide a tasty surprise.

1   10-ounce jar maraschino cherries (42 to 48)
½ cup butter, softened
1   cup sugar
¼ teaspoon baking powder
¼ teaspoon baking soda
¼ teaspoon salt
1   egg
1½ teaspoons vanilla
½ cup unsweetened cocoa powder
1½ cups all-purpose flour
1   cup semisweet chocolate pieces
½ cup sweetened condensed milk

Preheat oven to 350°F. Drain cherries, reserving juice. Halve any large cherries. In a medium mixing bowl beat butter on medium to high speed for 30 seconds. Add the sugar, baking powder, baking soda, and salt. Beat until combined, scraping sides of bowl occasionally. Beat in egg and vanilla until combined. Beat in cocoa powder and as much of the flour as you can with the mixer. Stir in any remaining flour with a wooden spoon.

Shape dough into 1-inch balls. Place balls about 2 inches apart on an ungreased cookie sheet. Press your thumb into the center of each ball. Place a cherry in each center.

For frosting, in a small saucepan heat and stir chocolate pieces and sweetened condensed milk over low heat until smooth. Stir in 4 teaspoons reserved cherry juice. (If necessary, thin frosting with additional cherry juice.) Spoon 1 teaspoon frosting over each cherry, spreading to cover cherry completely.

Bake for 10 minutes or until edges are firm. Let stand 1 minute on cookie sheet. Transfer to a wire rack and cool. Makes 42 to 48 cookies.

for the tin

Drill two holes near the center of the lid. Thread a chenille stem through one hole, through the loop in a large jingle bell, and back through the remaining lid hole. Twist the ends of the chenille stems together to secure. Tie a ribbon bow around the bell; trim the ends. Use alphabet stickers to spell out holiday wishes in tone-on-tone fashion around the lid edge.

Chocolate-Cherry Cookies

Chocolate Ginger Cutouts

Chocolate Ginger Cutouts

½ cup butter
4 ounces bittersweet chocolate, chopped
¾ cup packed brown sugar
1 egg, slightly beaten
¼ cup molasses
1 teaspoon ground ginger
¾ teaspoon baking soda
½ teaspoon ground cinnamon
¼ teaspoon ground cloves
2½ cups all-purpose flour
1 recipe Royal Icing
Decorative candies

In a medium saucepan combine butter, chocolate, and brown sugar. Cook and stir over low heat until smooth. Remove from heat. Cool for 15 minutes. Stir in egg, molasses, ginger, baking soda, cinnamon, and cloves until combined. Stir in flour. Divide dough in half. Cover and chill for 1 or 2 hours or until dough is easy to handle.

Preheat oven to 350°F. On a lightly floured surface roll half of the dough at a time to ¼-inch thickness. Using a 2½-inch cookie cutter, cut out dough. Place cutouts 1 inch apart on an ungreased cookie sheet. Bake about 8 minutes or until edges are firm. Transfer to a wire rack; cool.

Pipe cookies with Royal Icing and add candies. Makes about 30 cookies.

ROYAL ICING: In a medium mixing bowl stir together ¾ cup powdered sugar, 1 tablespoon meringue powder, and ⅛ teaspoon cream of tartar. Add 3 tablespoons warm water and ¼ teaspoon vanilla. Beat with an electric mixer on low speed until combined. Beat on high speed for 7 to 10 minutes or until mixture is very stiff, the perfect consistency for piping. Makes 1½ cups.

for the bag

135

Clear cellophane bags, available where cake decorating supplies are sold, become handy holders for single-serve cookies. To trim a bag, drill two holes in the top of a mini cookie cutter and thread with fine cord; tie the bag closed. Tie a larger ribbon bow around the top of the bag.

for the plate

 A small glass plate or candleholder is just the right size for a mini serving of meringues. Gem stickers create pattern and color around the rim.

Strawberry Meringue Stars

Strawberry Meringue Stars

Crisp meringues take a dip in melted chocolate for a flavor and texture combination that's truly spectacular. Keep the morsels the same size so they dry in the specified time.

- 3 egg whites
- 1 teaspoon white vinegar
- ⅛ teaspoon salt
- ¾ cup granulated sugar
- ½ of a 3-ounce package (about 3 tablespoons) strawberry-flavor gelatin
- 6 ounces bittersweet chocolate and/or white chocolate, melted
- Sifted powdered sugar

Let egg whites stand in a medium bowl at room temperature for 30 minutes. Line large cookie sheets with parchment paper; set aside. **Preheat oven to 300°F.** Add vinegar and salt to egg whites. Beat with an electric mixer on high speed until soft peaks form (tips curl). Gradually add sugar and the dry gelatin, beating until stiff peaks form (tips stand straight).

Spoon mixture into a pastry bag with a large star tip (at least ½-inch opening). Pipe stars, about 1 inch wide and 1 inch tall, onto prepared cookie sheets. Bake 18 to 20 minutes or until dry but not brown. Turn off oven; let meringues dry in oven for another 15 minutes.

Peel meringues from paper; let cool on wire racks. Decorate meringues, dipping bottoms into melted chocolate. Place on waxed paper until chocolate sets up. Sprinkle meringues with powdered sugar. Makes about 90 cookies.

TO MAKE AHEAD: Place undecorated stars in layers separated by waxed paper in an airtight container; cover. Store at room temperature up to 3 days or freeze up to 3 months. Decorate as directed.

Nutty Chocolate-Covered Caramels

Reserve some of these irresistible treats for your holiday candy tray. The caramels are also sturdy enough to ship long distances. Pictured opposite.

- 1 cup butter
- 1 16-ounce package (2¾ cups packed) brown sugar
- 2 cups half-and-half or light cream
- 1 cup light-color corn syrup
- 1 teaspoon vanilla
- 3 cups semisweet chocolate pieces, melted
- 1 cup finely chopped walnuts

Line an 8×8×2-inch or a 9×9×2-inch baking pan with foil, extending foil over edges of pan. Generously butter the foil. Set pan aside.

In a heavy 3-quart saucepan melt butter over low heat. Add brown sugar, half-and-half, and corn syrup; mix well. Cook and stir over medium-high heat until mixture boils. Clip a candy thermometer to the side of the pan. Reduce heat to medium; continue boiling at a moderate, steady rate, stirring frequently, until the thermometer registers 248°F, firm-ball stage (45 to 60 minutes). (Adjust heat as necessary to maintain a steady boil.)

Remove saucepan from heat; remove thermometer. Stir in vanilla. Quickly pour mixture into prepared pan. When firm, use foil to lift candy out of pan. Use a buttered knife to cut into 1-inch squares.

Dip each square into melted chocolate; sprinkle with chopped nuts. Let stand until set. Wrap each piece in waxed paper or plastic wrap. Store wrapped candies at room temperature up to 2 weeks. Makes about 2 pounds (64 pieces).

for the house boxes

A two-piece papier mâché house transforms into a snow-laden candy box in two easy steps. First paint the main house portion using acrylic paint; let dry. Paint the roof a contrasting color and sprinkle with chunky glitter while wet. Let the paint dry. Use paper or cellophane shred to stuff the bottom portion of the house before adding wrapped candy.

137

Nutty Chocolate-Covered Caramels

for the nest

Artificial nests, available in crafts stores, make unexpected treat holders. Create a snowy effect by painting the outer edge with white acrylic paint and sprinkle with glitter. When dry, line the nest with parchment paper or cellophane and clip a bird ornament to one side.

Milk Chocolate Sandwich Cookies

Assemble the cookie sandwiches just before you present the gift to the recipient so the cookies are fresh.

¾ cup all-purpose flour
¾ teaspoon baking powder
⅛ teaspoon salt
6 ounces 30- to 40%-cocoa chocolate or milk chocolate
3 tablespoons butter, softened
½ cup sugar
1 egg
¾ teaspoon vanilla
1 recipe Milk Chocolate-Sour Cream Frosting
White chocolate, melted

In a medium bowl combine flour, baking powder, and salt; set aside. In a heavy small saucepan heat the chocolate over low heat until melted, stirring constantly; set aside.

In a medium mixing bowl beat butter with an electric mixer on medium speed for 30 seconds. Add sugar; beat until fluffy. Add melted chocolate, egg, and vanilla. Beat until combined, scraping sides of bowl.

Gradually beat in the flour mixture. Divide dough into four equal portions. Wrap each portion in plastic wrap. Chill in freezer for 20 to 30 minutes or in refrigerator for 1 hour or until firm enough to handle.

Preheat oven to 350°F. Removing one portion of dough from freezer at a time, roll each portion into a 10-inch-long roll.* Cut each roll crosswise into ¼-inch slices. Place slices 1 inch apart on ungreased cookie sheets. Bake for 9 to 10 minutes or until edges are set. Let cool on cookie sheet for 2 minutes. Gently remove from sheets (cookies will be brittle) and transfer to wire racks to cool completely.

Spread ½ teaspoon of the Milk Chocolate-Sour Cream Frosting on half of the cookies; top with remaining cookies. Drizzle cookies with melted white chocolate. Serve the same day.

MILK CHOCOLATE-SOUR CREAM FROSTING: In a medium saucepan melt 3 ounces chopped 30- to 40%-cocoa chocolate or milk chocolate and 2 tablespoons butter over low heat, stirring frequently. Cool for 5 minutes. Stir in ¼ cup sour cream. Gradually stir in 1 to 1¼ cups powdered sugar to make of spreading consistency. Makes 144 tiny cookies or 72 tiny cookie sandwiches.

*NOTE: It helps to place the dough on a sheet of waxed paper and use the paper to help shape the roll. If dough becomes too sticky, return to the freezer for a few minutes.

TO MAKE AHEAD: Place unassembled cookies between layers of waxed paper in an airtight container; cover. Store at room temperature up to 3 days or freeze up to 3 months. Thaw cookies; assemble sandwiches as directed.

Milk Chocolate
Sandwich Cookies

139

Stamp It ▶

A stamped image mounted on coordinating papers makes a gift tag in an instant. Even the kids will love inking these tags. To make them pop, use adhesive spacers to lift the image from the backing papers.

In a Twinkling
tag you're it

◀ Pure Bling

Solid tags, available where scrapbook supplies are sold, come in all sorts of styles. To personalize one as a package topper, press on acrylic gem stickers in the shape of a letter.

▲ Pretty Punch

A border paper punch transforms plain paper into a filigree tag in seconds. Thread narrow sheer ribbon through one of the openings and label with a pen.

◀ Window to the World

Recycle holiday cards into clever gift tags. Choose those that have a small scene and trim to approximately 2½ inches square. Make window panes using a 1-inch-square punch and black paper. Adhere the layers together with glue stick and mount on card stock background.

▼ Tied with a Bow

Felt pads are created by machine stitching square and rectangle layers stuffed with a puff of batting. Hot-glue the packages to folded card stock, then use a sewing needle to poke holes on each side and thread with fine cording.

▲ Woven Wonder

Short lengths of ribbon make big impact woven into a pretty pattern. Hold the small weaving in place with packing tape pressed onto the wrong side of the ribbons. Mount the mini masterpiece on card stock to make a card-style tag.

INSPIRE *the* KIDS

Pretty papers, bright dyes, sparkling beads, and whimsical stickers lay the groundwork for crafts that kids are proud to share.

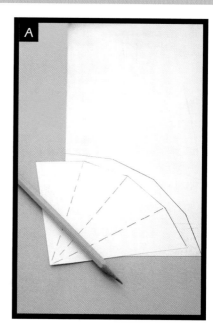

fun forest

Dimensional trees get a coat of wintry fun when shaped from colorful scrapbook paper.

paper trees

Crafting a tabletop forest is as easy as trace, cut, fold, and glue. Make the trees for a dresser top or as the centerpiece for Christmas dinner and let everyone enjoy your creations.

1 Trace the tree patterns on page 157; cut out. Keep in mind the solid lines on the pattern are cut lines and dotted lines are fold lines.

2 Trace around the pattern on the wrong side of the card stock as shown in Photo A. Use a ruler to draw fold lines from the point of the tree to each of the 3 lower angles as shown in Photo B. By drawing in solid fold lines, the paper will crease easier.

3 Cut out the card stock tree shape.

4 Fold the tree along the three drawn lines as shown in Photo C. Overlap the edges and glue in place with a glue stick.

5 Use crafts glue to attach a pom-pom to the treetop.

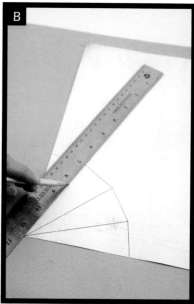

to dye for

Tie-dyed and edged with vivid trims, this pillowcase infuses bedtime with color and fun.

colorful case

Combine fun tie-dye and simple machine sewing to make a supercool pillowcase.

147

What You'll Need...

- white pillowcase
- rubber bands
- tie-dye kit with desired colors of dye
- metal pan
- rickrack and ribbons to coordinate with dye colors
- thread

1   Fold the pillowcase in half lengthwise. Accordion-fold the case approximately every 4 inches as shown in Photo A. Secure the folded case with rubber bands as shown in Photo B.

2   Work over a metal pan to protect the work surface. Wear plastic gloves and follow the manufacturer's directions to dye the folded pillowcase as shown in Photo C.

3   When dye process is complete, wash the pillowcase and let dry.

4   Carefully machine-sew rickrack at the edge of the case opening. Stitch stripes of ribbon to cover the case edge, folding under ribbon ends when stitching.

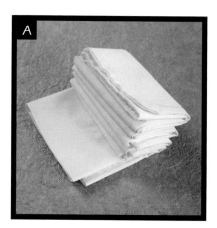

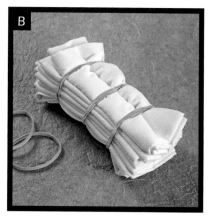

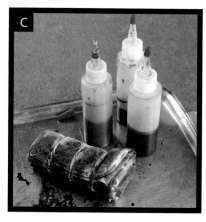

backpack charm

Add a splash of style to a backpack with colorful charms dangling from the strap.

beaded bobble

 Beaded wires and photo charms filled with decorative paper add whimsy to a plain backpack.

What You'll Need...

- [ ] scissors
- [ ] decorative paper scraps
- [ ] photo charms
- [ ] heavyweight crafts wire
- [ ] wire cutters
- [ ] beads with openings large enough to fit wire
- [ ] round-nose pliers
- [ ] ball chain

1. Cut decorative paper to fit into photo charms. Place paper pieces into charms.

2. Use wire cutters to cut three lengths of wire, each approximately 6 inches long. Slip a charm on each wire and use round-nose pliers to curl wire end to secure charm on end.

3. Thread each wire with beads, leaving at least 1 inch of wire unthreaded. Curl each wire end using round-nose pliers, leaving a hole large enough to accommodate a ball chain.

4. Thread the beaded pieces onto ball chain and hook onto backpack strap.

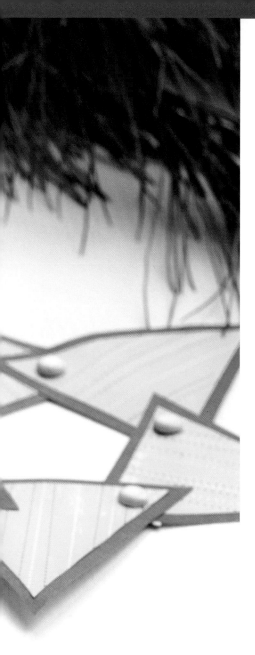

so starry

Connect paper triangles with brads to make movable stars.

candle ring

〜 Whether placed under pillar candles or hung from thread, layered paper stars lend contemporary flair to holiday decorating.

1 Trace the triangle patterns on page 158; cut them out. Use a paper punch to make the pair of holes on the small triangle pattern as shown in Photo A.

2 Use the patterns to cut 5 large triangles from solid paper and 5 small patterned triangles from patterned paper as shown in Photo B. Mark the 2 punch holes on the right side of each small triangle piece.

3 Glue each small triangle piece to a larger one as shown in Photo C.

4 Punch holes where marked. Overlap triangles as shown in Photo D, using brads to hold the pieces together.

Silent Night ▶
Make or purchase card
stock note cards. Add a
sticker scene and an
alphabet sticker message to
a plain paper band glued
to the card front.

In a Twinkling
stuck on stickers

◀ **Dinnertime Delights**
Whether guests are on the
way or it's just the family
tonight, make the table
festive with cheery place
cards. Place a label on
folded card stock and trim
a narrow border. Add a
matching punched circle
and dimensional sticker
detail. An alphabet sticker
identifies each place setting.

153

◄ Too-Cute Tags

Frame stickers with layers of card stock to make gift tags for family and friends. Apply the fun paper pieces to folded card stock and the tag is ready to write.

Favor Jar

A single sticker transforms a small jar or candleholder into a treat jar in a jiffy. Tie ribbons on the handle and fill with candy to make a joy-filled favor.

◄ Advent Tree

Colorful papers cut to fit metal-edge tags create a fun background for adhesive numbers on one side and stickers on the other. Number the tags for each of the 24 days of Advent. Hang the trims on a mini tree with all of the numbers revealed. As each trim is flipped during Advent, it reveals a sticker image and appears as a fully decorated tree come Christmas.

project details

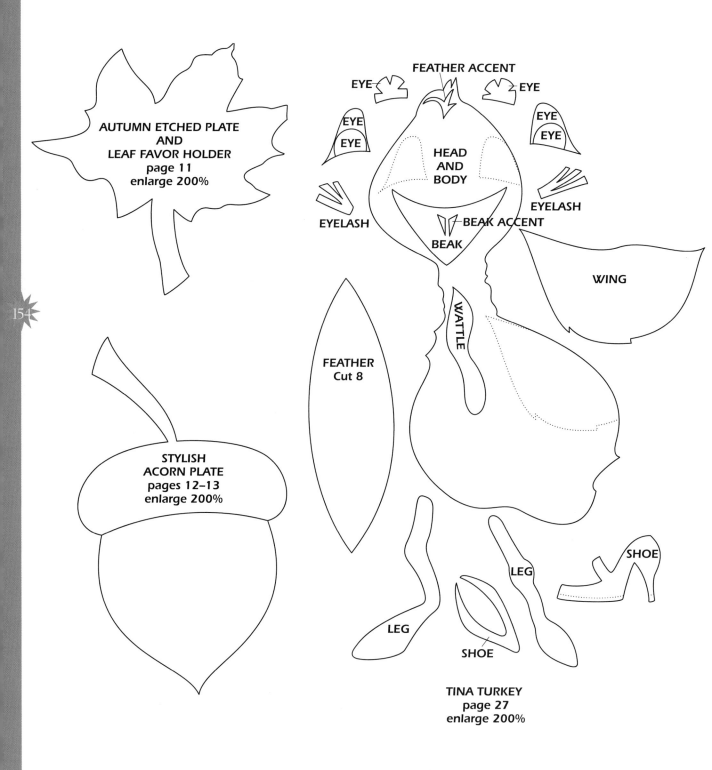

AUTUMN ETCHED PLATE
AND
LEAF FAVOR HOLDER
page 11
enlarge 200%

STYLISH
ACORN PLATE
pages 12–13
enlarge 200%

EYE

FEATHER ACCENT

EYE

EYE

EYE

EYE

EYE

HEAD
AND
BODY

EYELASH

EYELASH

BEAK ACCENT

BEAK

WING

FEATHER
Cut 8

WATTLE

SHOE

LEG

LEG

SHOE

LEG

SHOE

TINA TURKEY
page 27
enlarge 200%

154

AGE REVIVAL
pages 8–9
enlarge 200%

FRENCH KNOT

LAZY DAISY

RUNNING STITCH

BLANKET STITCH

JOLLY PAIR FELT ORNAMENT
SNOWMAN
page 49
enlarge 200%

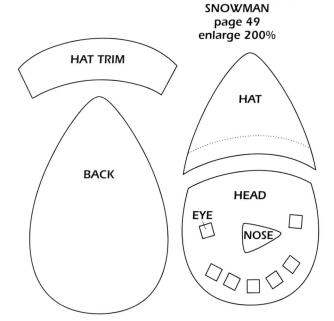

HAT TRIM

HAT

BACK

HEAD

EYE

NOSE

JOLLY PAIR
FELT ORNAMENT
SANTA
page 49
enlarge 200%

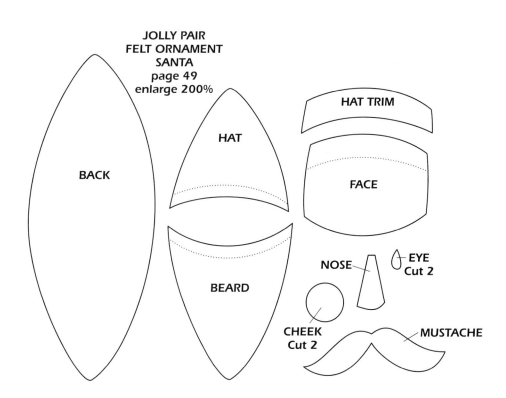

BACK

HAT

HAT TRIM

FACE

BEARD

NOSE

EYE
Cut 2

CHEEK
Cut 2

MUSTACHE

155

continued

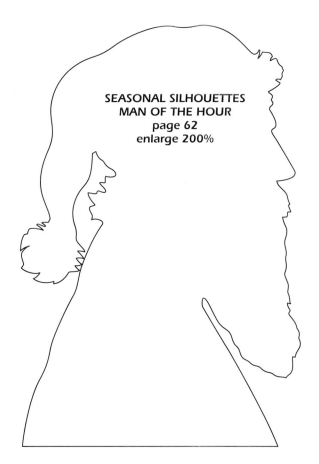

SEASONAL SILHOUETTES
MAN OF THE HOUR
page 62
enlarge 200%

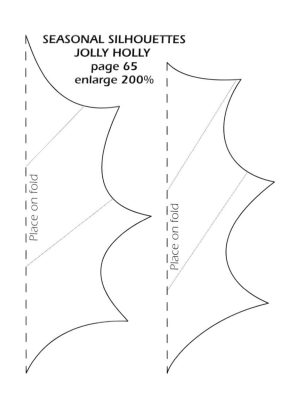

SEASONAL SILHOUETTES
JOLLY HOLLY
page 65
enlarge 200%

Place on fold

Place on fold

SEASONAL SILHOUETTES
BERRY NICE
page 63
Full-Size Patterns

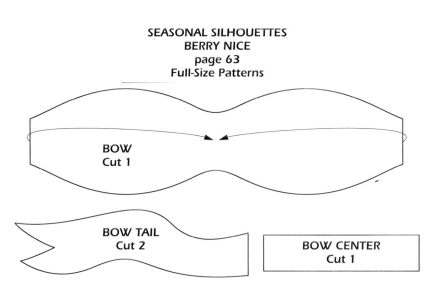

BOW
Cut 1

BOW TAIL
Cut 2

BOW CENTER
Cut 1

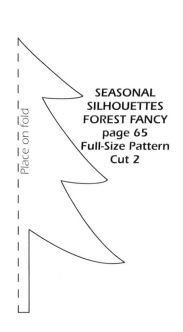

Place on fold

SEASONAL
SILHOUETTES
FOREST FANCY
page 65
Full-Size Pattern
Cut 2

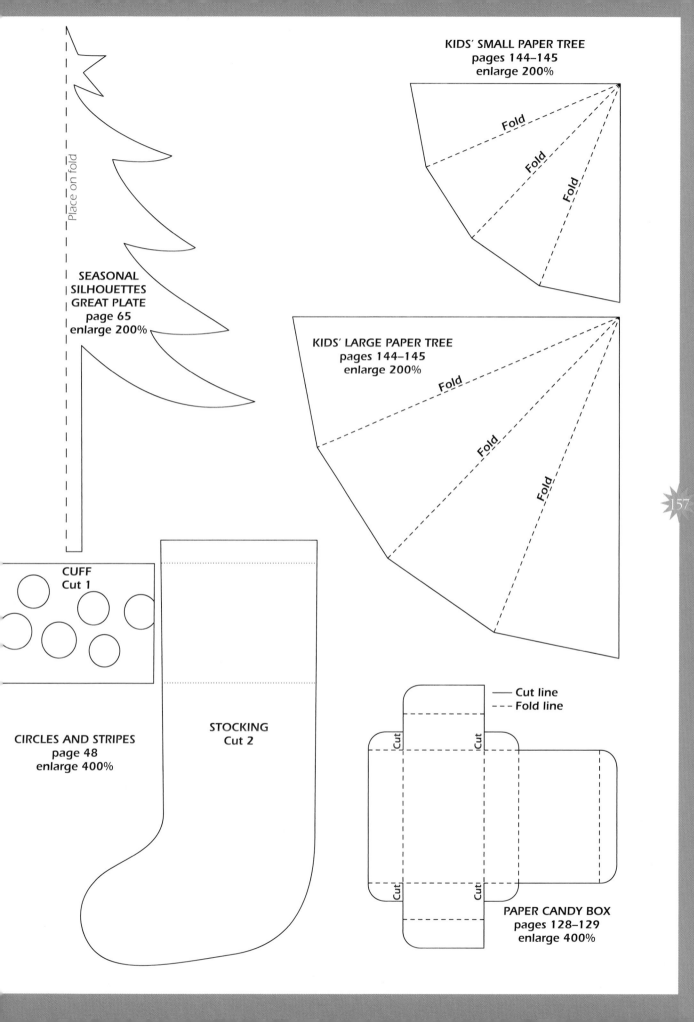

KIDS' SMALL PAPER TREE
pages 144–145
enlarge 200%

Fold

Fold

Fold

Place on fold

SEASONAL
SILHOUETTES
GREAT PLATE
page 65
enlarge 200%

KIDS' LARGE PAPER TREE
pages 144–145
enlarge 200%

Fold

Fold

Fold

CUFF
Cut 1

CIRCLES AND STRIPES
page 48
enlarge 400%

STOCKING
Cut 2

Cut line
Fold line

Cut

Cut

Cut

Cut

PAPER CANDY BOX
pages 128–129
enlarge 400%

157

continued

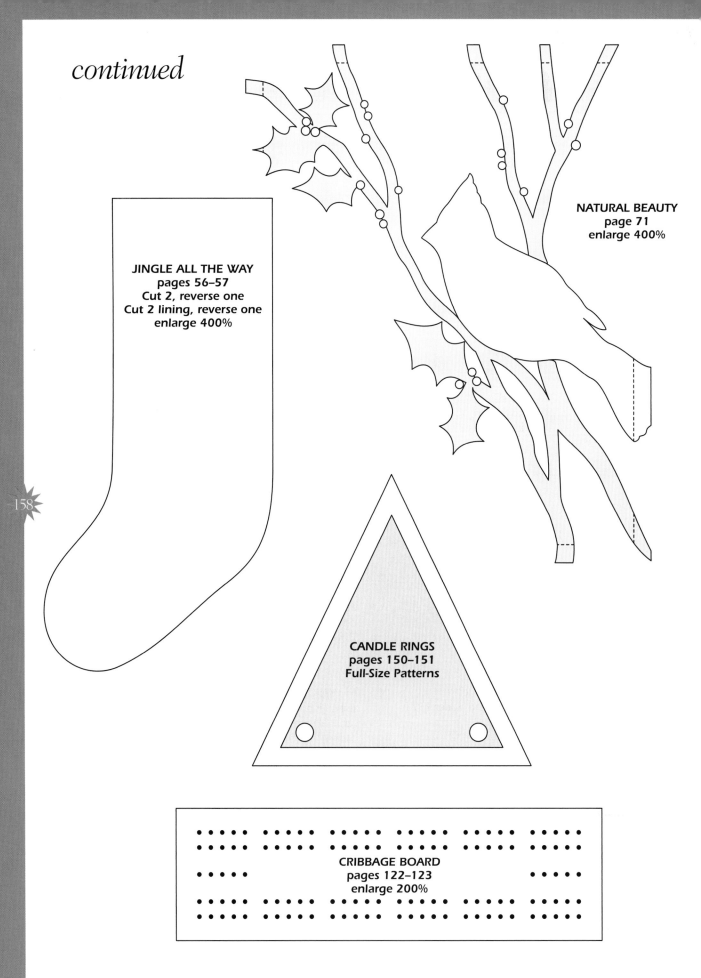

NATURAL BEAUTY
page 71
enlarge 400%

JINGLE ALL THE WAY
pages 56–57
Cut 2, reverse one
Cut 2 lining, reverse one
enlarge 400%

CANDLE RINGS
pages 150–151
Full-Size Patterns

CRIBBAGE BOARD
pages 122–123
enlarge 200%

index

index *continued*

160

CREDITS & SOURCES

PHOTO STYLING
Crafts and decorating—Sue Banker
and Catherine Brett

Food—Catherine Brett

PHOTOGRAPHY
Marty Baldwin
Jason Donnelly
Scott Little
Jason Wilde

FOOD STYLIST
Charles Worthington

PROJECT DESIGNS
Sue Banker

SOURCES
Pages 10 and 39—Leaf plate and
candy jar etching cream by Armour
Products, 176-180 5th Avenue,
Hawthorne, New Jersey 07506.

Page 13—Wood plate by
Walnut Hollow, 1409 State
Road 23, Dodgeville, WI 53533;
walnuthollow.com.

Page 17—Wood slice by
Walnut Hollow, 1409 State
Road 23, Dodgeville, WI 53533;
walnuthollow.com.

Page 59—Ornament decoupage
medium by Plaid Enterprises, Inc.,
PO Box 7600, Norcross, GA 30091-
7600; plaidonline.com.

Pages 71 and 73—Canvas painting
and ornament acrylic paint by
Plaid Enterprises, Inc., PO Box
7600, Norcross, GA 30091-7600;
plaidonline.com.

Pages 86–87—Leaf metallic paint
by Plaid Enterprises, Inc., PO Box
7600, Norcross, GA 30091-7600;
plaidonline.com.

Pages 122–123—Cribbage board
wood sign by Walnut Hollow,
1409 State Road 23, Dodgeville, WI
53533; walnuthollow.com.